A Writer's Garden

For Sarah —
Best Wishes —
[signature]

Love,
ANGELA

"For more than 30 years Ethel Pochocki has been sowing garden seeds: stories and verse that have colored the inner landscape of generations of readers. In A Writer's Garden we find a breathtaking selection of her new and previous plantings. Within this volume are sights and fragrances to fill our senses. And there are lessons here, too, between the rows and the roses. This is a book that will make every reader grow in wonder and delight."
    —Linus Mundy, publisher at Abbey Press, and author of *The Complete Guide to Prayer Walking and Slow-Down Therapy*

"It has been said that genius is a matter of making connections. If this is true, as I suspect it is, then Ethel Pochocki is most certainly a genius. She is a writer who notices everything. Not only does she notice, but she studies and reflects and connects, especially in her garden. There, and in her kitchen making jams and salads, she finds Mystery and Holiness — God, if you will — within the quotidian: an oak tree in a celery stalk, umbilical stars in apples, and the Trinity in a green pepper. Here is a no-nonsense, frugal, pragmatic and unsentimental writer who focuses her prodigious powers of observation on the garden behind her house in rural Maine, and laces those observations with her knowledge of myth, music, life, literature and fable to inform and shape the poems, prose, and fairy tales that comprise this wonderful book called A Writer's Garden."
    —Barry Moser, author, illustrator, lecturer, botanist

"At long last readers will catch a brief, but illuminating, look at the private and spiritual world of beloved writer Ethel Pochocki. I began to collect her work in the late 1970s, and though I read her children's books and many of her essays in magazines and The Christian Science Monitor, nothing prepared me for the breadth and depth of her writing. This little book renewed my spirit and gave me a sense of the hope and promise of each new day. In the chapter entitled 'Fringe Benefits,' Ethel declares that 'there should be a special word for the osmosis of beauty!' I think there is, and that word is Ethel."
    —**Sharon Lovejoy**, author and illustrator of *Sunflower Houses, Hollyhock Days, Roots, Shoots, Buckets & Boots, Aphid Wolves and Willow Water*, and contributing editor to *Country Living GARDENER* magazine.

"Ethel Pochocki writes with humor and sensitivity, and just and occasional twinge of exasperation, about the bumtious glories of her garden — which she views as a 'stage upon which the drama of life, from birth to death and the journey between, is played out.' Strutting across the stage of A Writer's Garden is a memorable cast of vegetables and flowers — seed pods bursting with life and rife with possibility. Her stories about cabbage moths and cabbages, about ladybugs and pea pods, about prickly blackberry brambles and even pricklier thistles will delight readers of all ages. And her poetry is exquisite — each poem a perfect distillation of wisdom and insight, and a catch-in-the-throat surprise. 'Sunflowers' send chills down my spine, while 'Elderberry Jelly' draws me to ponder the essence of a life lived 'to a full rolling boil.' I've been a fan of Ethel Pochocki's writing for many years, and this collection of poems and stories reminds me of just why that is."
    —Deborah Vetter, executive editor, CRICKET and CICADA

A Writer's Garden

Ethel Pochocki
Illustrated by Peter LaGue

FOREST OF PEACE
Publishing

Suppliers for the Spiritual Pilgrim
Leavenworth, KS

Also by the Author:
(available from Forest of Peace Publishing)
The Mistletoe Girl and other Christmas Stories

A Writer's Garden
copyright © 2002, by Ethel Pochocki

All rights reserved. No part of this publication may be reproduced or transmitted in any form or by any means, electronic or mechanical, including photocopy, recording, or any information storage or retrieval system, without permission from the publisher.

Library of Congress Cataloging-in-Publication Data

Pochocki, Ethel, 1925-
   A writer's garden / Ethel Pochocki ; illustrated by Peter LaGue.
     p.cm.
   ISBN 0-939516-61-6 (pbk.)
   1. Gardening—Literary collections. 2. Gardens—Literary collections. 3. Gardening.
 4. Gardens. I. Title.

PS3566.O25 W75 2002
813'.54—dc21

2002022799

published by
Forest of Peace Publishing, Inc.
PO Box 269
Leavenworth, KS 66048-0269 USA
1-800-659-3227
www.forestofpeace.com

printed by
Hall Commercial Printing
Topeka, KS 66608-0007

illustrations and cover design by
Peter LaGue

1st printing: March 2002

"Ladybug's Garden" appeared in CRICKET in May 1990, "Five in a Pod" appeared in CRICKET in April 1999, and "Faux Fruit" appeared in CICADA in March/April 2000. "The Late Bloomer" and "True Love Never Dies" were first published in *Soup Pot* by Resurrection Press, Mineola, NY, 1996.

Dedicated to

Elizabeth of Hungary,
dear saint of bread and roses

Connection

*I bought the jar of honey
at the discount store
for a dollar
can't go wrong,
honey is honey,
I tell myself,
besides, the jar is pretty,
a honeycomb on its lid,
small, just right
for summer jam*

*at home,
the label informs me
that this honey
was made by bees
in a Hungarian meadow,
and joy warms through me
like a sudden blast of sun*

*I stand in the winter
kitchen,
waist high in waving poppies
and yarrow and paintbrush,
I know this place
and the young girl running
barefoot through it,
blonde curls and a necklace
of white clover heads
streaming behind her*

*she is that ancestor
I know only through
my mother's remembering,
along with tales
of family noses and tempers
and an uncle who trained
Lippizaner horses*

*I have formed her
in admirable image,
wise child, wise woman,
who has given me my love
for earth and words,
I see her, older now,
moving with soft feet
and careful eyes
in this very meadow,
foraging flowers and herbs,
stripping willow bark and cherry,
to use as poultice
or potion to discourage
moths and fitful sleep,
bending, weaving
in gentle dance,
courteous of the bees
whose descendents carry on*

*from my mother's gold-rimmed cup,
I drink the honeyed tea,
in communion with all
who have made me,
the child with bouncing curls
and those who came before her
who dance in my heartbeat,
ride the rapids in my
tributaries of blood,
tantalize my mind
with impudent violins,
seize my fingers
with laughter
as I type*

*bless all of you
who hover around my cup
and speak to me of family!*

Contents

1. A Writer's Garden..................8
   - From the Deck..................11
   - Thinning Corn..................12
   - Ladybug's Garden..................13

2. Volunteers..................16
   - The Upstarts..................19
   - Indian Relish..................19
   - The Poppy Angel..................20

3. November Daffodils and Good Friday Peas.....24
   - Green Friday..................27
   - The Fragrance of Lilac..................28
   - Life After Life..................29
   - The Cabbage Moth and the Shamrock..................30

4. Outwits and Stratagems..................34
   - Faux Fruit..................37
   - Cabbage Moths..................38
   - Thoughts on Pro-Life..................38
   - The Woman Who Wanted a Little Zucchini....39

5. Useless Beauty..................42
   - Foxglove..................45
   - Horsechestnuts..................45
   - Mrs. Yap-n-Snap..................45

6. Celestial Design..................48
   - Design by Accident..................51
   - Red Cabbage..................52
   - The Star at the Heart of Things..................53
   - Five in a Pod..................54

7. Lessons from the Berry Patch..................58
   - Blackberry and Thistle..................61
   - Elderberry Jelly..................63
   - The Gypsies' Tale..................64

8. Fringe Benefits..................68
   - Pomander..................72
   - Pressing Cider..................73
   - Wildflower Tea..................73
   - Hercule and Dijon..................76

9. The Perfect Bouquet..................78
   - Meddling..................81
   - Sunflowers..................81
   - Still Life..................82
   - The Late Bloomer..................82

10. The Garden in Winter..................84
    - The Whiteness of Meringue..................87
    - Random Alignment..................88
    - Iceflowers..................89
    - True Love Never Dies..................90
    - Recycling..................92
    - The Fruitcake..................93

If there is anywhere on earth where metaphor flourishes and parables abound, it is in the garden — any garden, any size, from the formal, impeccably laid-out estate to the humble, everyone-welcome cottage jumble, from postage-stamp city backyard plots to fire-escape containers and window boxes bursting with parsley and pansies.

For me the garden is a parallel world. According to the *Encyclopedia of Science Fiction*, a parallel world is "another universe situated alongside our own, displaced from it along a spatial fourth dimension." The idea that we connect with a parallel world is "one of the oldest speculative ideas in literature and legend."

But this universe of the garden is not in some unseen, somewhere-in-time dimension. We can see and smell and touch it — this stage upon which the drama of life, from birth to death and the journey between, is played out. Here the virtues (faith in the unseen, hope, trust, compassion, tolerance, patience, steadfastness) are put to the test, and weaknesses (greed, envy, anger, neglect, sloth, indifference) are illumined. Here on this battlefield, in this schoolroom, courtroom, sanctuary of healing, we dig for ethical solutions; we compromise, try to do no harm, accept defeat with grace and triumph with modesty — and, always, as Emily Dickinson puts it, we "dwell in possibility."

Each day, as a new episode in this living theater unfolds, nothing happens that does not mirror the circumstances and struggles of our human life. With the delicious anticipation of a writer coming to a blank sheet of paper, we plant the seeds and seedlings in the freshly-tilled soil. We hover over them, feed and water them, uproot the smothering weeds, all in faith that dreams will become reality, all the while knowing they may not.

Some seeds will rot in the ground; others will sprout and die young because of drought, mildew, cutworms or marauding bands of critters and bad bugs. Still, we do our best, work until bones and back rebel, and trust that all will be well. We pray to St. Isidore the farmer for guidance in our daily crises, how to discourage the convention of flea beetles on the broccoli, how to keep the night-raider raccoons out of the corn, rabbits out of the peas, birds out of the cherry trees.

Even though the just-war argument may be acceptable and easier, I prefer to outwit rather than kill. But I admit there are moments of desperation when I would cheerfully eliminate the enemy. Do I resort then to traps or poison? Or do I learn to live with the Mexican bean beetle and hope there's enough for both of us?

Then there's the matter of volunteers, those plants who spring up without invitation from the dormant seeds of last year's bounty or who come by wind or bird or God's joke. They set up camp and settle in for the duration, brashly, blithely depending on the gardener's hospitality. I once had an invasion of poppies, a glorious pink army marching through and into the rows of beans and cabbages. Who was I, I thought, to snuff out these plucky survivors because they disturb the order of things? Shouldn't all visitors "be received as Christ," poppies included?

I am just as ambivalent about thinning corn, a chore I heartily dislike. I feel like a Nazi officer in a concentration camp decreeing which prisoners shall live, which ones shall die. Yet I know thinning is for the common good. On the other hand, couldn't the Nazis, in their warped obsession for a "pure" race, have used the same argument, "for the common good"? Weary of inner debate, I look for loopholes, tell myself that thinning is like triage, where doctors on the battlefield must choose to help first the wounded most likely to survive. If I don't thin, the seedlings will crowd each other out and grow poorly. And so I thin, leaving a trail of limp, green bodies along the way. Playing God isn't easy.

Reflecting God *is*, and I believe we do that when we create our gardens. The urge to make something of beauty where there had been nothing is imprinted in our royal genes. It is no wonder that when Jesus, the master storyteller, came to teach us, he gave us homely parables about gardens and vineyards, figs and thistles, mustard seed and barley. Long after we read them as children, these stories have stuck with us in their clear, unpretentious simplicity.

We pay attention to Jesus' message, "Look at these growing things, learn from them, see yourselves!" And so we make our gardens and grow our own crop of parables.

From the Deck

my son built a deck
out back behind the dining room,
for safety, he says, an escape
in case of fire

such practical awning
gives ample shade
for larger truth,
that exit yields entrance
to a parallel realm,
where benevolent lorelei
proffer heaven
in the known

where roughwood floor
is royal box
and rocker is my throne
from where I command
the world carry on,
I am here!
commence the feast!

there's larksong and thistledown
spinning on whim of wind,
animal games played out
in wit and war and circus ring,
crusader beetles crossed with gold

plodding to Jerusalem,
butterflies by Tiffany,
fireflies miming the Pleiades,
raucous crows screeching demands
for better-class garbage,
the dervish dance of aspen leaves,
the measured procession
of wise old clouds,
linked one to one like elephants,
unreeling in slow-motion glory
into wispy-bearded shadows
of selves

from my wicker throne
I survey my domain
of metaphor,
review the parade
of parable,
gather up the fragments
to feed me
later

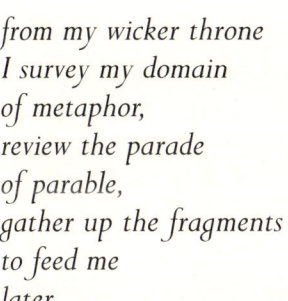

Thinning Corn

today
I play God,
deciding
which ones live,
which ones die,
which seedling side by side,
each of equal unknown promise,
will give the greatest yield
and thus inherit the earth

in an eyeblink
I judge,
and the one perhaps
a hairbreadth shorter
or of paler green
I uproot with robot precision,
leaving a trail of limp young bodies
to fertilize the row

it is the work of the day,
nothing personal,
it is for the common good
so the chosen ones may grow
strong and healthy,
with every row of golden kernels
uniformly perfect

why then,
as I wash my hands,
do I feel like a commandant
at Auschwitz,
deciding
which prisoners live,
which prisoners die?

Ladybug's Garden

There once was a young ladybug who lived in an old bookstore inside a book called *The English Flower Garden*. She had not planned to live there, but because of the sudden, sad circumstance of losing her parents, it was the best she could do.

She had been quite happy living with her parents high on the shelf in their winter home of *Webster's International Unabridged Dictionary*. There she had spent happy days becoming a well-educated ladybug and had, right up to the tragic moment, already memorized 122 word definitions.

But then the terrible thing happened: The dictionary was sold, and the ladybug's parents went out of her life forever. She herself had slipped out of the book, sliding down on the letter tabs, and was waiting on the shelf for them. But they never came. They were gone forever.

The book that sat next to the dictionary was almost as fat and heavy. It seemed safe and comfortable. Its edges were quite worn and the lettering faded, but the ladybug could still read the title: *The English Flower Garden*. She crawled up onto the front cover, then over the top edge into the book itself. Fortunately, the cover was loose, so she could travel easily within the pages.

Before she knew it, she found herself on the table of contents and she began to read: "Castle Gardens," "Cottage Gardens, "Bog Gardens," "Alpine Climbers," "Flowering Shrubs" — why, this could be a lovely home! She could learn about the flowers her parents had once promised she would someday see. And there were pictures, she discovered excitedly, drawings of the gardens and forests and terraced castles and thatched-roof cottages.

Slowly her sadness wore away as she traveled the gardens of England page by page. One day she sat amidst the primroses and Canterbury bells of Fillingham Castle, the next in a cottage garden of hollyhocks at Winchfield, Hants. Another day the ladybug sat under palm trees on the Cornwall coast, and she rang foxglove bells in Somersetshire. Each day brought its own adventure.

Although she learned their names and where they grew, the ladybug could not truly know the flowers, for all the pictures were in black and white. And she couldn't smell them, only read their descriptions and imagine their sweetness or sharpness as she imagined their color. She knew she lived in a black-and-white world that was not the real thing. Still, it was what she had, and she was grateful for it.

The ladybug might have spent her life pleasantly within these pages if the book had not been sold. One day a woman put her gloved hand around *The English Flower Garden* and lifted it from the shelf.

"Oh, I can't believe this," she cried softly. "I've been searching for years for a copy. My grandmother had one, and I remember visiting her and sitting in a swing and reading all about the flowers in Lady So-and-So's garden! I'm so happy to find it!"

I'm very happy for you, thought the ladybug, but what's going to happen to me?

The bookseller wrapped the book up. For the moment, the ladybug was safe, but what would happen when the woman began flipping through the pages, reliving her childhood memories page by page? The ladybug could become homeless — or worse — in a matter of seconds.

When the woman arrived home, she put on the tea kettle and began to peel away the brown paper with shaky fingers. She sat down in the rocker by the window and laid the book carefully in her lap. She opened it to the table of contents, and she began to smile and sigh. It was just as she remembered it. Meanwhile, the ladybug was safe and snug within Chapter XL: "Alpine Flowers, Rock and Wall Gardens."

Then came a flash of black-and-white fur, surprising the woman. She shrieked and dropped the book.

"Drat you, Max!" the woman muttered angrily to the cat, who hissed and growled back at her. "Look what you've done. If any pages of this precious book have come loose, you'll be punished." The cat looked past her as if she were not there and began to wash his ears.

The woman poured her tea, picked up the book and sat down once more in the rocker. The ladybug, shaken loose from her rock garden, had fallen deep into the pile of a rug patterned with swirls and scrolls of ivy and flowers. For a moment, she thought she had been dropped into a garden, the colors were so rosy warm and bright. But no, it couldn't be, for all the flowers smelled the same — musty and not too pleasant. She started to follow a scroll as if it were a path, when she felt a dark shadow fall over the rug-flowers. It was Max, coming toward her in a quiet crouch.

He was a young-enough cat to think anything that moved — a mouse, a leaf, a bug — was an enemy to be chased and caught. He came close enough for her to count his whiskers, and then he sprang. In her fright, the ladybug spread her wings and flew blindly into the air. This was her first flight, and her sense of direction was poor, which is why she landed on the cat's back.

Max was furious. He couldn't see behind him, but he knew something was walking down his spine onto his tail. He danced around and around until the ladybug grew so dizzy, she couldn't hold on. Once again she flew up in awkward circles and landed on an herb wreath hanging on the wall.

She caught her breath, resting for a moment on a sprig of faded lavender. She knew these plants, the silver sage and pearly everlasting of the meadows, and she liked the faintly woodsy smell. But there was a dust-and-brittle feel to them all, with as little life as the black-and-white drawings. No, she thought sadly, this might have been a garden, but it was a very dead one now and it didn't suit her.

Max had disappeared into the kitchen and was trying to get into the silverware drawer, which the woman had left open. The ladybug crawled down the wallpaper of roses and peonies onto the fireplace mantel, over pictures in silver frames, down the bricks of the fireplace and back onto the floor.

Then she smelled something so sweet, it almost hurt her to breathe. It was coming from the top of a table by the window where the sun was streaming in. The ladybug flew up and landed in a saucer. Could it be the tea, she wondered? She made her way around the rim of the teacup carefully — one slip and she would find out if she could float or not — but the tea's fragrance, although pleasant, was not what she had smelled.

She scurried, at her ladybug pace, to the blue china bowl sitting at the edge of the table by the window and scaled the side, which was quite slippery. When she reached the top, she gasped.

Here was a garden to rival any in the book! On a bed of water and white pebbles and periwinkle shells sat three bulbs wrapped tightly in their dowdy brown shawls. Their long stringy roots had settled down to the bottom of the bowl, where the shells sang softly of their lost ocean home. From the hearts of the bulbs grew tall green stems topped with heads of frilly red petals. They towered above the ladybug as did the palm trees of the Cornwall coast.

And, oh, the smell! She crawled up each stem and went into the scarlet tendrils until she felt quite drunk and had to come down to rest in their shade.

She was at that moment utterly content in her garden of red hyacinths. At last, she was mistress of a real garden of quiet stream and pebbled path and petaled trees. Here she would bask in the sun and see beyond the window to the blue sky and the chestnut tree and the spirals of mint and sweet peas just breaking through the earth. Perhaps someday, when the window was opened…. But for now, she asked no more.

Oh, she would have enjoyed the company of her parents or another ladybug, but one couldn't have everything.

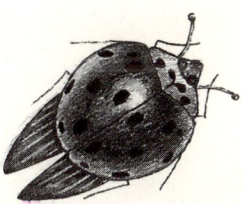

Volunteers of any variety can be blessing or bane. I'm not speaking of those we seek out, those who come running when we need help, but those who arrive on our doorstep and disrupt our well-laid plans — the unexpected visitor, the unexpected child, the unexpected stranger who knocks in the dead of night. I call them volunteers because that is what we in Maine call the unexpected strangers that make their home in the garden without invitation or encouragement.

We also know them as intruders, invaders and *those horrid weeds*. Some have local roots, are descendants of last year's zucchini and tomato crop hibernating in the compost. Others are gypsies who come by whim and wind — poppies, tansy, buttercups, mallow, thistle — carpetbags in tow, eager to set up camp in this pleasant summer resort.

I watch the stealthy invasion in its zigzag march across my orderly rows. Annoyingly, they seem stronger, more luxuriantly green than my fussed-over seedlings. They have the impudence of the street urchin living on the edge, daring the authorities to stop him. The poppies soon tower over the pea patch in brazen scarlet beauty; yet, generously, they offer themselves as support for the young vines. I cannot bear to pull them up because their blooms are so beautiful. Tolstoi said the world would be saved by beauty. The world, perhaps, but not my peas.

And so I struggle with the question of which is more important: the love of beauty or the love of peas. Uncurtailed, the poppies would besiege the garden completely, so I have made an arrangement that turns this bane into blessing. I let them have their moment in the sun, until the petals fall, then immediately uproot them before the seed pods dry and progeny escape. I gather the stalks for a neighbor who turns them into Christmas angels. With their round pod

faces, crown-tipped in gold, thistledown hair, wings of dried grasses and long white gowns of gauze, they preside regally over all the housebound Christmas trees in the village. A grand fate for carefree lilies of the field!

There is the lemon tomato volunteer that shouldered its way up between the bean rows, an awesome thing whose leaves shaded everything within its circumference. Let it be, I thought, even though the sight of it annoyed like a picture hanging crooked on the wall. I had no premonition that some animal would eat the legitimate tomato plants right down to the ground and that the stranger would be the lone provider for summer salads. The night before the first killing frost, I picked every green plum-shaped fruit and used them, along with peas and apple culls, to make green tomato mincemeat. And so there were mincemeat pies for Christmas and jars of it to give away as gifts. All because I let the stranger stay.

There is the mystery pumpkin that grows every year without my planting it. But I do know its origin. After Halloween each year, the jack o'lantern goes out to the garden, crammed with seeds as winter treats for mice. Eventually, the face begins to sag, scowly eyes dissolve into each other, and it finally collapses into a soggy orange mess. The snow comes and mercifully covers all; yet one seed escapes, makes a bed and sleeps till spring, when it wakes to repeat the cycle. Always the vine grows in a different place, and always it bears just one perfect pumpkin.

I have come, gradually, to look beyond these disturbances to my controlled world and to see the good in these volunteers. It's all a matter of attitude. (Is the glass half full or half empty?) I may choose to look upon them as evil robbers hiding, in their Trojan horse of beauty, waiting to ravage my innocent, neat garden, or I may entertain them as angels unaware, who teach me how to live with risk and to be open to the unknown.

I see them too as natural sacramentals, those tangible markers of faith (holy water, oil, bread, statues) that "outwardly signify something spiritual, something symbolic of the unseen and eternal." Sacramentals remind us of the spark of God that lies within every living thing, and in that spark, however layered in disguise, is goodness.

So when I consider the jars of mincemeat standing so spiffy on the shelves, the poppy angels protecting their trees, this Halloween pumpkin, candle burning bright within, casting deliciously spooky shadows on the walls, I relish the blessings that have come from a little sacramental disorder.

The Upstarts

three gypsy buttercups
invade propriety,
set up camp among
delphinium and lupine,
their leaf so similar,
who could tell?
and with their brazen
brash of gold
against the purple blues,
who would mind,
save the gardener overruled
by divine disorder?

Indian Relish

she goes to the store and buys
cat food, coffee, green grapes,
half a pound of Swiss
and one sweet red pepper.
the pepper is for making relish,
which she does because there is
a plentitude of tomatoes,
and because she always has,
even though the children never liked it,
and the friends who did are gone,
and a little goes a long way
when you're alone

still, in the kitchen
washed in twilight sun
and lingering vinegary spice,
the regiment of jars
standing so spiffy on the shelf
makes her pilgrim proud,
comforts her against the winter,
like the old days

Volunteers • 19

The Poppy Angel

In a garden of beautiful flowers, there grew a poppy who thought herself the most beautiful of all — and, in truth, she was. She was tall and strong, towering above her sister poppies and foxglove and sweet william and larkspur. Her purply scarlet satin petals were double ruffled, like petticoats under a dancing gown. She was the only one of her kind. Where she had come from or what mischievous wind had brought her was a mystery.

The poppy stood out, catching every eye, and she reveled in being the center of attention. She had no false modesty about this. "I am beautiful beyond compare," she preened proudly as the wind ruffled her petticoats.

"But I am stronger than you," teased the wind, "and I can make you dance, whether you like it or not!"

The poppy only laughed because she knew better. "Oh blow away, you old thing," she teased the wind right back. "I shall dance, but only if I choose."

> *I will not bow,*
> *I will not bend,*
> *My beauty is such*
> *It has no end!*

The other flowers shook their heads at her boldness, but they were not jealous, for despite her high opinion of herself, the poppy had a kind heart. If she acted like an elegant queen, she was a merry and generous queen as well. She welcomed all to her court — whether birds, bees, butterflies, hummingbirds or an occasional inchworm who crawled into her petals to take a nap. As long as they paid her proper respect, she enjoyed them all.

Unfortunately, the queen's reign was not long. The scarlet petals turned dull, curled up and dropped off. The poppy looked quite different now. She was still tall and strong and green, but with the petals gone, her face could be seen. It was round and full as a doll's chowder bowl, and a crown of thirteen stars sat upon her head. Now she looked like a jolly, middle-aged queen who no longer thought of being fashionable.

The wind howled around her gleefully and tried to make her bend and bow, but she would not. "Just wait a few weeks when you're brittle and brown," he laughed, "you won't be so proud then, my fine lady! You'll be just like the rest of them."

That time did come, when leaves began to fall and nothing remained flowering in the garden but wild clover and Michaelmas daisies. The smaller poppies huddled together, shivering in their nakedness and whispering quietly among themselves, their crowns head to head. Soon, they gossiped, they would be picked to be used in dried bouquets, along with the milkweed pods and cattails from the swamp.

The poppy listened and shrugged. She knew that would never happen to her. She would not bend and she would not bow and she would never be stuck in a bunch of anything. She was not, after all, just another poppy.

Before any of the flowers was picked, a young woman came into the garden from out of the woods. She had been gathering grapevine for wreaths and hops for sleep pillows that she would sell at autumn fairs. She was tall and strong and wore a long red dress and a straw hat with a wide brim. The poppy watched her with approval. She was almost as lovely as the poppy had been in her youth.

The young woman stopped by the garden and gazed at the proud poppy stalk. "Well, look at you," the young woman smiled, "you're extraordinary. I've never seen such a round face…. Someone should do something with you."

As the woman stood there, the sun, the golden sun of September afternoons, came through the trees in thin fingers of gold and bathed the poppy in a shimmery light, and she seemed to have a halo over her crown.

"An angel!" exclaimed the young woman. "You're an angel!" She knew right then and there what she would do with the poppy. She snapped the dry stem, shook the seeds from the round pod into her hankie, tied the ends together tightly, stuck it into her dress pocket and carried her treasure home.

Late into the night she worked, trying to make the poppy into the vision of the angel she had seen in the garden, until it finally came right. By dawn, her eyes were heavy, her fingers sore, her body stiff, but her spirit was giddy as a bubble, for her angel was finished.

The poppy-stalk body had been swathed in layers of cotton to fill her out, and over this hung a gown of gauzy cheesecloth, which the young woman had dipped into beet juice to make it a deep purply crimson. A shawl of the same color was tossed lightly around the angel's shoulders. Her arms, which reached out in loving welcome, were made of wire and covered tightly with white gauze and bound with thread, as if she were wearing long white gloves.

Golden wild grasses drooped from her shoulders in the shape of wings, and driplets of hardened wax, like the winter dew, clung to the lacy ends. Her face and crown were framed in a halo of milkweed down. As the morning sun shone through the window onto the angel, the young woman thought she had never seen a more heavenly sight.

She tied a small golden string where the two wings met and hung the angel from a nail above the window. As she drank her morning coffee, she sat and admired it and wondered what she would do with it.

At first, she thought she would keep it; she could not bear to part with it. But then, like a mother with a newborn baby, she yearned to show off her creation and hear exclamations of delight over her offspring. She decided she would bring the angel to the craft fair — just to show, not to sell.

And so she did. As she knew they would, the people flocked around her stall admiring and wanting to buy the angel, but she would not sell and the people moved away. One gentleman did not go. He stood quietly before the angel, never taking his eyes off it, his thumb under his chin, his forefinger tapping his lips.

Finally he spoke. "I know you do not want to sell your angel. If I had made such a magnificent thing, I would not either. But, would you consider sharing it with others who need her beauty — children and old folks and sad folks and people who don't have gardens? Someplace where she would live forever and be treated with great care?"

The young woman was quite puzzled by all he said. He explained that he was the head of a museum in a large city, where every year a gigantic Christmas tree was mounted in the hallway, right in the center of spiraling marble staircases and crystal chandeliers. On this tree were hung priceless ornaments from every corner of the world — glass swans from Germany, wooden clowns from Sweden, homespun cornhusk dolls from Kentucky, straw doves from Mexico, snow globes that played music....

"And at the top," he said, "under the star, would hang the poppy angel. Not just this year, but every year. She would live forever. Or reasonably close to that."

"Say yes!" yearned the poppy angel. She very much liked the idea of again being the center of attention and holding court in a new garden. She was, of course, grateful to the young woman for having transformed her, but she certainly didn't want to live in that dreary cottage forever.

The young woman hesitated, for she was torn between keeping and sharing, but she finally agreed, for she was not a selfish person at heart. The gentleman paid her handsomely and also bought a grapevine wreath for his wife and a sleep pillow for his train ride home. The young woman wrapped the poppy angel in layers of tissue paper, packed her into a sturdy box for carrying and bade her farewell.

She was sad to say good-bye to the angel, but under the sadness, she felt a smile. She reached in her dress pocket for the hankie with the seeds she had shaken from the poppy's pod. She would plant them this very day for spring blooming.

As the gentleman had foretold, the poppy angel drew all eyes to where she hung on the magnificent Christmas tree. The poppy, no more humble as an angel than a flower, was not surprised. She had survived wind and frost and old age. She had not bowed or bent or been picked to gather dust in dried bouquets with teasel and Japanese lanterns and other old relics. Now she reigned again.

"Of all the beautiful ornaments on this tree," she preened in absolute contentment, "I am the most beautiful of them all."

Her pride was an honest, not boastful, one, for the beauty she had been given had been returned wholeheartedly to praise the Christ child in the crèche. Because of him, she had reason to live again.

In truth, the poppy with her gift of self, the young woman with her gift of seeing and her skill in making it real, and the gentleman with his gift of wisdom, all gave praise in a manner worthy of such pride.

Rosemary, says Shakespeare, is for remembrance. I would add, so too are Good Friday peas and November daffodils, for they are a remembrance that birth and death are bound together in a seamless circle of resurrection. We can't have new life without some form of death.

In November, traditionally a month reserved for the Holy Souls, death is daily with us. The lush green leaves of summer now crumble brittle beneath our feet. Skeletal trees stretch gaunt, pleading limbs to heaven, and the garden lies silent within its brown shroud. Yet, here and there dotting the landscape, there are the hunched-over humans planting daffodils in tombs six inches deep. The foolish optimists believe that no matter how fierce the winds and storms of winter, these innocuous bulbs, humble peasants in their brown baboushka shawls, will grow and multiply and, come spring, erupt into an explosion of golden joy as miraculous as the first resurrection.

This fall, my friend planted a hillside with 100 daffodils. As she entombed each bulb, she offered a prayer — for a loved one who had died, for living family, children and friends. Then she spread her prayer out to heads of state, starving children, the homeless, the lonely elders, for peace in the Middle East, a cure for cancer, the melting of unforgiving hearts within families. In this small act of connection, she felt she was truly a part of the Mystical Body.

But that springtime glory lies hidden now in the long sleep of winter. Spring here in Maine is a reluctant, cranky recluse who won't be prodded awake. (We often bypass it and go directly to summer.) No matter the weather, however, for Christians spring begins on Good Friday when we plant a symbolic row of peas. I don't know the origin of this custom — Nordic, Celtic, Eastern European? — but it seems a right and proper thing to do on this day.

Between noon and 3 P.M. we poke a row of holes into the unreceptive, often frozen earth. Sometimes we must crack the ice on top with a screwdriver, if our stiff blue fingers can't penetrate. Sometimes, if Easter is late, the soil is so muddy that the seeds disappear with a slurp.

Anyone watching us must think us fools. In the eyes of the rational world, we are, for we are obviously blind to implausible impossibilities. What do you expect of those who believe in a young woman made pregnant by the Holy Spirit, of a King who chooses to be born in a stable, who dies and won't stay dead, and who in his great-hearted love promises us the same? *Of course*, those who believe in such things are capable of planting peas in snow.

St. Therese says that God answers our prayers according to the measure of our confidence. So we confidently, faithfully, plant peas in the worst of weather in honor of Christ's resurrection, certain that they will produce yards of greenery and pods crammed with pearls of nourishment. We bury bulbs in winter, confident that they will push through in spring like Wordsworth's host of daffodils "beside the lake, beneath the trees, fluttering and dancing in the breeze" and that their fragrance will rise on the wind like Benediction incense to heaven.

How this happens is mystery, and mystery, like grace, leavens life with wonder. We have nothing to do with it; it will happen whether we will it or not. It is a gift we should accept with delight and let it go at that.

Our small human brains try so hard to explain and dissect mystery, as if by doing so, we may give respectability to our faith. Yet mystery by definition cannot be defined. What scientific formula, what philosophical deduction, can pinpoint the molecule of life within a pea seed or the trigger for laughter, or explain why grass is green instead of burgundy?

What human mind can divine the Divine?

Green Friday

on this dark and bloody day,
it is the custom
to plant peas,
to plant them no matter
if the earth be mud
or glazed in ice,
to plant them in sleet
or thunder or flinty wind,
fumbling with frozen fingers
for just enough soil
to cover the shrunken pellets,

all the while knowing how it seems,
the sublime absurdity of it,
the affront to reason
and horticultural certainty,
and paying it no mind,
for on what more propitious day
do we play the fool,
proclaim the paradox
of shroud as cocoon
hiding mystery,

until the wrapping falls away,
runs off with that old liar death,
and the green heart
bursts into a glory of tendrils.

The tomb is empty,
the thorn in flower.
God's in his heaven,
and we shall have peas.

The Fragrance of Lilac

the lilac bush
leans against
the barn door,
almost unnoticed now,
past its moment in the sun,
the pyramids of purple curls
faded, weepy, spotted with rust;
now peonies await applause,
roses waiting in the wings

yet its fragrance
denies the present,
does not linger
gently in reminiscence
of glory days in May,
but it rides strong on the wind,
assaults me, stops me
in my tracks,
with an elegance so sharp,
so piercingly sweet,
it cuts my breath in half

what alchemy connives
to outwit age
in this gone-by bush?

what churns in the bowels
of roots, up the highway
of veins, out the flowering pores,
to paralyze so sweetly
with perfume the white-coated
chemists struggle to imitate
in laboratory beakers?

as with other
unfathomables
ever within grasp —
children, hummingbirds,
the complexity of cabbage heads
and cats' minds —
the fragrance of lilac
is a mystery of the ordinary,
a sacramental leading
to deeper mystery

Life After Life

the apple tree is dead,
felled by January ice,
a toppled obelisk
sunken by its weight
into the earth

yet now in May,
blossoms of mottled pink
adorn the unleaved limbs
like rouge and powder
on a corpse

is this burst of beauty
a quirk of timing,
like hair and nails
that grow on in the grave,
the brain dismissed,
having left them
on their own?

all I know is
here are sweet fresh flowers
to warm my heart
later the fragrant motherwood
will warm the rest of me

The Cabbage Moth and the Shamrock

There was once a cabbage moth named Fiona, who was sadly plain and dull-looking. She was not beautiful, as one might expect a Fiona to be, with large wings swirled in orange and yellow, with black stripes and dots of white. Nor did she cause people to catch their breath in delight to watch her flutter by, up and up into a blue August sky.

Rather, she was very small and pale, with not a whit of color to turn an eye. She looked as if she had spent her life in the shade. The only attention she received came in sudden sharp voices of exasperation from ladies tending their gardens. "Drat that moth! Watch it, there she goes! Quick, kill her before she gets to the cabbages!"

Fiona got to know that tone and would head immediately for the low-lying white briar roses in the field, where she would stop quivering and lay flat on the petals and try to get hold of herself. She would stay there while the ladies sought out snails and squash bugs and other enemies before finally going inside to check their blueberry pies in the oven.

Fiona was timid as well as plain. If she had fingernails, she would have chewed them. And she had no talents to speak of. She could not spin a web and catch the morning dew in a rainbow. She could not rub her legs together and make music as the crickets did in the fall or sing a treesong as the spring peepers did. She was not able to light up the sky in a sprinkle of fireworks as fireflies did on a June evening, nor could she make honey from wildflowers as her friends the bees did.

What she did mostly was chew holes in cabbages, not because she was a bad moth but because it was her nature to chew holes in cabbages. When she was not doing this, she sat by herself and thought a lot. She had few friends, and most of these were other undesirables whose aim in life was to eat, hide and not get caught.

There was Maeve, the green broccoli worm, who had a sour disposition because of her nervous stomach. She never knew when the bud she lived in would be picked and she would be thrown into an icy brine to curl up and die — or, if she escaped the briny bath, be boiled and served with butter on the broccoli. Conrad the Snail and Drusilla the Cornborer were passing acquaintances who lived in different worlds, but at least they greeted her civilly and did not turn away from her with a wrinkled nose.

In contrast to her narrow, uninteresting existence, Fiona yearned with all her heart to be a breathtaking creature. For underneath her quiet, drab surface, she was a real Fiona, a dazzling, fiery queen, a Monarch who rippled the air with sweet wafts of honeysuckle and wild cranberry blossoms. The outside Fiona always smelled faintly of sauerkraut. The inside Fiona sought out beauty wherever she was. She explored the shell of a periwinkle and listened to the echo of her soft hello. She sat for an hour on the sleeve of a red velvet dress hung out for a spring airing, sinking into its deep lush redness with joy. She hovered about a little girl who had come into the garden to play her flute for the fairies and danced and danced as the notes hit the sky like crystals.

She wanted so very much to add to the world's beauty, to be brilliant, to be admired. She thought wistfully that she would even wish to be loved. But although she might be shy and plain and a dreamer, she was not dumb. She knew the facts and she accepted them. So she worked at being contented with what she had, a hard enough job, and she held onto her name to keep her heart light in dark times. Oh, how she loved her name! Just suppose it had been Bertha, or Hermione, or Mildred, or Soggybottom. The very thought of it made her count her blessings.

She did have one friend outside the bug world who was very dear to her. His name was Jeremy, and he was a shamrock, one of a bunch living under the purple apple tree. She had met him one hot July afternoon when she was being chased by an angry lady with a flyswatter.

She was flying in wild, fearful circles when he snapped, "Down here, quick! Under the bramble leaf!"

He had saved her life, for the leaf was so large it draped itself over the shivering white wings, and the lady stormed away, unable to find "that pesky thing." Fiona thanked Jeremy, and they told each other their names. They agreed that they were exceptionally lovely and suited each other perfectly.

"Fiona...it is delicate and graceful and airy. It is a small white fairy with red hair and a gypsy wit," said Jeremy.

"Jeremy...one with such a name is gentle and brave, a gentleman and a scholar, kingly but humble," said Fiona.

"I like a butterfly that isn't bold or gaudy, always showing off as if she owned the world and clashing with the colors of flowers. Oh, how that hurts my eyes!" said Jeremy. "You are pure as the first snow, and no matter what flower you touch, you add to its brilliance, like a poppy or scarlet snapdragon, or you bring out its softness, like a daffodil or larkspur." Fiona did not tell him that she was not a true butterfly and that she lived among coarse cabbage leaves. She loved him too deeply to take away his illusions.

"I love your green. It is so alive and full of hope and cheer, no matter what. You're sure of yourself without being arrogant. You have the manners of a prince and the simplicity of one close to the earth," said Fiona, happily adding up his virtues.

And so they spent the summer of contented days and nights in each other's company. They shared the sweet smell of wheat cut to hay and the music of quiet winds ruffling the aspens. They survived the constant dangers of predatory humans, greedy birds, heavy rains, drought, small children with heavy feet and butterfly nets and scythes. By late September, when the mellow chants of the crickets had replaced the happy questions of the May peepers and August katydids, Jeremy's green had faded and was tinged with spots of brown. He did not stand as princely tall as when Fiona first found her true love.

And Fiona's wings fluttered more slowly each day. She shivered now more with the fall chill than with delight over the trill of a flute. They knew that changes would be coming to their life soon, but they would not think of them now, this minute. They would continue to delight in the fact that, by God's good grace, they had found each other at all.

One day a high, blustery wind carried Fiona away from Jeremy over the tops of goldenrod and purple asters, onto a tuft of sailing milkweed down. It whirled them through spirals of sky and then suddenly, sharply, to earth, onto a clump of oak leaves already dried out and crinkly by the side of the road. Fiona lay still and unmoving on her puff of down. She was dead. The silky strands of milkweed enveloped her in the shimmery pale beauty of a royal princess asleep.

Before she could be squashed by a boy riding down the road on a bike, or a horse, or a dog chasing a squirrel, Fiona was found by an old lady. She had been limping along the road, her eyes squinting and searching for whatever might please her. When she came to Fiona, she stopped and smiled, and a hundred wrinkles made roadways on her face. She picked up Fiona and her bed of down and laid her gently in the basket over her arm. She passed through the plumes of goldenrod and hobbled through the grass gingerly, as if in pain. She paused by the gnarled apple tree still heavy with small purple apples, rummaged below it and picked two apples and a handful of peppermint sprigs. Then she came to the clump of shamrocks, bent down, picked Jeremy, and laid him in the basket next to Fiona.

She made her way back to the road and followed its curve, stopping now and then to ease her pain and to pick a few hazelnuts for the pocket of her brown sweater or to look up at the geese honking their way across the sky.

She came soon to a small red house with a black and white cat named Max sitting on the step. Max rubbed against her legs and wound his tail in and out of them. She put her basket down on a wooden table inside the house and poured Max some milk from a can into a chipped, blue bowl. Then she emptied the contents of her basket onto the table, and peace came over her face and excitement into her eyes.

She went over to a box labelled SCRAPS – FEED BAGS and took out a small rough piece of burlap. She brought it to the table, along with scissors, a pot of paste, crayons and a cigar box of odds and ends. She began to cut and paste and snip and draw, until the sun, which had shone brightly through her little window when she began, grew dim and the reflection of the setting sun glowed warm and pink on the pane.

At last she stopped, rubbed her eyes and put her hands on her lap. Max jumped up on the table and purred, "Yes, yes, that is very nice, my dear mistress; now would you have a bit of liver sausage for me, perhaps?" She lifted the burlap so he might not hurt it with his jumping and tacked it onto the wall with two rusty thumbtacks.

She fed Max one half of a cold sausage and ate the other half herself, took the two apples and the handful of hazelnuts out of her pocket and put them on the table. Then she unwrapped a hard heel of pumpernickel bread from its brown wrapper and made a cup of peppermint tea.

She sighed with contentment...how rich were today's gifts!...and admired her handiwork on the wall.

On the burlap she had drawn with green crayon a border of ivy leaves, attaching Jeremy at the bottom, with Fiona poised directly above him, as if ready to alight. Above them she had printed:

LIVE IN THE JOYOUS
MIRACLE OF NOW!

Under the protecting arch of NOW! Fiona and Jeremy had been reunited and would live forever, as all true lovers do. They showed that everything God has made can give a joy unable to be measured. Even a cabbage moth and a shamrock.

We like to consider our gardens as a source of refreshment, a refuge from other realities, where we soak up sun and warmth and solitude. But the illusion of a never-changing natural Utopia is quickly dispelled once we encounter the problems of maintenance.

Among the maxims on my refrigerator door, two tackle the problem of problems with no-nonsense forthrightness. One is by writer John Gardner: "We are all continually faced with a series of great opportunities brilliantly disguised as insoluble problems." The other wise saying is by cantankerous H.L. Mencken: "For every problem, there is a solution that is neat and simple — and wrong."

These might seem contradictory — no matter how hard we try, we are probably wrong — but I find them comforting and complementary. Try as we might to do what is right, we may not find perfect solutions; yet we keep on, plunging anew into the next disguised great opportunity.

Nowhere are these opportunities so abundant as in the garden, for no garden is an island. There will always be the wants of others that collide with ours. In our human world, we may hide from or deny irksome relationships, but there's no escaping them in the garden. If you don't deal with them, the garden will die.

The "others" here are the animals and insects who would destroy the gardener's winter dreams and turn the mildest pacifist into a raging killer. Pesticides, traps, bombs, poison, anything will be considered to keep the sanctuary healthy. What is hard is that we have the choice to do this. We can accept plummeting meteors, other people's wars, plagues, pestilence because we must. They are out of our control. But in daily matters on our plot of the universe, we are stewards who have the power of decree.

Outwits and Stratagems

My decision is to follow the advice of Hippocrates to his medical students: "First do no harm." But although I don't want to kill anything or poison my portion of earth, I would also like to enjoy a few meals from the fruit of my labor. Bugs and critters vs. the nonviolent peacenik. How do I solve this insoluble problem?

I try to outwit my adversaries. I reason that my human intelligence outsmarts theirs, although each year I grow less sure of this. I read, I listen, I ask questions, I experiment with my own strategies. I concoct nontoxic sprays unpleasant enough to drive the freeloaders to relocate. Every year I discover new surefire remedies that have gradually merged into one, a bit of this, a dash of that, in varying ratios of what I have on hand: apple cider vinegar, garlic, salt or Epsom salt, baby shampoo and baby oil, cayenne pepper, tea, beer. I spray the plants while the morning dew is still upon them or after a rain or whenever I see the fluttering clusters of cabbage moths, whose larvae drill cabbage leaves into lace.

I "plant" banana peels and orange rind around the garden edge and matchstick heads (for sulphur) with the roots of broccoli, coffee grounds with carrot seed to discourage maggots. I sprinkle wood ashes around newly planted seedlings to protect them from cutworms. I practice companion planting: garlic with roses, nasturiums with beans, marigolds with cucumbers, horseradish with potatoes. I plant pumpkins in the corn row, so the raccoons, who like to savor their stolen bounty standing up, will trip over the vines and leaves and lose their balance. (I admit to enjoying this image. I'm not perfect.)

I make use of weird and intriguing devices, equivalents of NO TRESPASSING signs, to convince the invaders that mine is the garden from hell. When I try to imagine the people who invent these amulets, I see them as a bit squirrely and beady-eyed, perhaps previously employed by the C.I.A. or the National Institute of Mental Health.

Some contraptions I categorize as versions of *The Emperor's New Clothes*, whose results we are to take on faith, such as the Electric Mole Repeller, which "sends out vibrations to send pests fleeing in fear," or the Natural Mole Chaser, a windmill that creates "underground disturbances moles can't stand," and the Night Molechaser, which "drives away menaces with a hideous sound inaudible to humans but unbearable to rodents." (What is audible is the sound of mole laughter.)

There are all manner of fake owls, such as the Glitter Owl, my favorite, cut from a metallic substance that shimmers and throws prisms as it waves in the wind, and the Rotating Head Great Horned Owl, which "gives the illusion of life," and the Prowler Owl, which hoots when it senses movement and has a 4" wingspan that flaps.

And there's the black metal Scaredy Cat that I have nailed to the top of a lattice for pea vines. As I work, I have the uneasy feeling he is following me with his roll-around marble eyes, and I am back in my childhood church with the statue of the Cure D'Ars, who never lets me out of his fierce gaze. And there's the "Aeolian" standing chimes that guards the lettuce bed, and the florescent angel chimes that glint spookily in the night. I once had the idea to paint the statue of St. Francis so he too would glow in the dark, but the phosphorescent paint came only in Hunter Orange and Lime Green, and I couldn't do that to Francis.

I've created a scarecrow out of a wooden cross planted in the center of the garden, clothing it in dresses (changed weekly) of wildest red flowers found at the Salvation Army. Crows have given it a wide berth, but it is a magnet for hummingbirds.

All in all, it is an interesting-looking garden, and I thank God it is behind the house and cannot be seen from the road. But has it worked? For the most part, yes. I have no doubt the "others" have gotten their share, but I have always had enough for summer eating and winter freezing and to give away to the visitor of the day.

My solution is not neat or simple or brilliant. It is one of accommodation and inclination, and it suits me. I can live with eating lacy cabbage.

Faux Fruit

(from the viewpoint of the maggot) "Red spears hung on blossoming trees are visual traps to confuse the apple maggot into thinking they are real fruit, and the pests get mired in the goo." —*Gardener's Supply Catalog*

as if things aren't bad enough,
having to tunnel away
our precious lives
(albeit work is sweet),
never knowing the moment
of demise

will death come
on the rack of cider press?
by hornet's lethal divining?
housewife making applesauce?
cattle who swallow us
into their bellies?

now this:
how shall we teach our young and giddy,
strangers to prudence,
that not all beauty is truth,
that this scarlet bauble is no more
than Snow White's poisoned apple?

it is discouraging,
but we will find a way

Cabbage Moths

they come like mystics
unannounced,
without publicity
or playbill,
blithe spirits rounding
the peripheral corner
to confound the unprepared
with wonder

hovering like hummingbirds
above the cabbages
in whispery clumps
that move as one,
none scouts ahead
or lingers behind

*flitting
in skittery indecision,
like teenagers in the mall
sampling perfume and cheese,
or little girls
in their fluttery
white communion veils,
eager to taste
the mystery*

so pretty,
so innocent,
so deadly in their
irrevocable worming
of leaf to lace

ah well,
there's always sauerkraut

Thoughts on Pro-Life While Contemplating Zucchini

I suppose
a rose the color
of coursing blood,
satin warm
as newborn skin,
is appropriate
as symbol of those
who would proffer life,
yet, when you turn your back,
the petals fall and wither
and that is that

I would think
the humble zucchini,
evergreen as hope,
biblically eager
to increase and multiply
(and multiply),
should more rightly
fly the colors
of exuberant
proliferation

The Woman Who Wanted a Little Zucchini

There once was a woman who one morning in the middle of winter decided she must have a zucchini for supper. She absolutely, positively, had to have it. There it was right on top of her head, this craving for one sweet, tender, sliced thin and sprinkled with butter zucchini — maybe with some Parmesan cheese. Just one little zucchini. All day long she could think of nothing else. It was one of those strange things that happen when you've been snowed in too long.

"I will have to buy one," she sighed, shuddering a little at the thought, for the old woman was a frugal soul who pinched pennies so fiercely you could hear them screaming inside her purse. She was a person who made do, patched up or went without. Almost everything she bought was day-old or second-hand. And she *never* gave anything away.

So the idea of buying a zucchini was unsettling. Yet so strong was her desire that she counted out 25 pennies into an old mustard jar, dropped it into her purse, put on her boots lined with newspapers and went on her way to the grocery store.

She headed right for the vegetable section, and her heart gave a little leap. There it was — one small zucchini, a rather old, shriveled one, but it would do. She carried it to the counter and said to the grocer, "Mr. McCormick, this zucchini looks a bit poorly, don't you think? Perhaps you'd like to get rid of it. I'd be willing to take it off your hands for, say, a quarter."

The grocer sighed and shook his head, for he knew the woman was digging in for a haggle, and he didn't have the energy for it. "I know it's not the best, but it is winter, you know. I've got to get 75¢ for it at least."

"*Seventy-five cents*! That's ridiculous! Why, I could never eat it at that price." The old woman's lips tightened and trembled. The line of customers behind her grew restless.

The grocer, whose cheeks were turning red, said, "Why don't I just give you this zucchini, ma'am. It would be my pleasure."

"Done," the woman smiled triumphantly and dropped the zucchini into her purse. Then she went on her way, chuckling over how very clever she was.

That evening, she sliced and chopped her bounty into a blue enamel pot, carefully setting aside three seeds she had scooped out from the center. As she held them in her hands, a quiet excitement grew within her, for she had a thought which turned into an idea which turned into a plan. She would plant those seeds in the spring, and then she would have her own fresh zucchinis all summer long.

She thought about this as she ate her zucchini, boiled, sliced thin, buttered, with a dash of Parmesan cheese. It tasted heavenly, and it hadn't cost her a cent! And for the rest of the winter, she dreamed of the marvelous crop she would have next summer.

Finally the bitter winds turned gentle, the snow went away for good, and the air smelled of earth and new green grass. The time had come. She planted the seeds in a place where the sun always shone. And then she waited.

One wonderful hot day in July, it happened. She found and picked the first baby zucchini, so small it still had part of the blossom attached. How different it was from that limp excuse of last winter. She almost purred with pleasure as she ate it in her salad.

From that day on, she ate zucchini every day. She had zucchini pancakes and zucchini omelets for breakfast, zucchini minestrone and zucchini quiche for lunch, zucchini goulash and zucchini meat loaf for supper, and zucchini brownies for dessert. And even zucchini pizza for a snack.

She canned 28 quarts of zucchini in tomato sauce and won a Blue Ribbon for her zucchini relish at the Labor Day Fair. What she did not eat herself, she sold to neighbors without gardens or at the stand in front of her house.

Of course, what with picking and grating and chopping and cooking and baking and selling all day, she had little time to go to rummage sales or berrying or clamming. Nonetheless, she could say with pride that not one zucchini was ever wasted.

Eventually, as often happens with too much of a good thing, people tired of zucchini *anything*. Now, at end of summer, they yearned for apples and cranberries and sauerkraut. And in her heart, the old woman admitted she too was tired of zucchinis.

But the zucchinis, who didn't care if they were wanted or not, just kept coming up in her garden. New ones sprouted every second of every hour of every day.

At night, the old woman couldn't sleep for wondering what to do with them. She sat in her rocker, zucchinis piled around her like armies ready to take over, and she thought and thought. Soon an idea sprouted inside her head as quickly as the seeds had in the garden.

The next morning she arranged all the zucchinis according to size, wrapped them in pairs, put them into boxes, and sold them at her stand as shoes. Mothers snatched them up, since children outgrow shoes so quickly, and a farmer with size 13 feet bought several pairs which fit him exactly.

The day after, she piled the zucchinis into the wheelbarrow and went into town. She sold them all to the manager of the bowling alley to use as bowling pins.

The next day she carved smiling and frowning faces on all the chubby, squat zucchinis, wrapped them in flannel blankets, and sold them as dolls to children who didn't care if they had arms or legs.

Then she dried the small zucchinis, filled them with lentils, painted them orange and sold them as maracas. She filled the middle-sized ones with kidney beans, painted flowers on them, and sold them as doorstops.

When the circus came to town, she sold them to the ringmaster, who shot them out of a cannon in an act called *The Flying Zucchinis*, which was a smashing success.

Finally, she ran out of ideas. What was left of the zucchinis the woman piled into a bushel basket and put it in front of her house with a sign: FREE! TAKE ALL YOU WANT!

The mailman carried off most of them for his pigs. A neighbor took one for her End-of-the-Garden Relish. A large dog, blind in one eye, carried off another, no one knew why.

Now only one squishy, turning-grey zucchini was left. The old woman threw it onto the compost pile and breathed a sigh of relief. She had learned her lesson. She would never, ever have anything to do with zucchinis again. She couldn't imagine whatever had possessed her to crave such a dull, foolish vegetable.

What she really wanted, right this moment, was a pot of steaming red cabbage, cooked with apple and onion and caraway seed and vinegar. Yes, that's what she wanted, a hearty vegetable strong with character — oh, she could taste it right now!

And as she yearned and dreamed of the rows of red cabbages she would reap next year, the seeds of the rotting zucchini stretched and yawned and snuggled deep into their soft dark blanket of compost and settled in for their winter sleep, until the first warmth of spring would rouse them and bring them up into new glorious life.

Useless beauty is always suspect. Its credentials are vague. What is it good for? What can you do with it? It's all very nice to delight the eye, but does it feed us or clothe us or provide a remedy for hiccups? What is the point of beauty that has no practical purpose?

The better question is: How could anything God creates be useless? In everything, garden and beyond, whether we understand it or not, there is purpose and a plan. In the slow-motion unfurling of a rose, the fragrance of lilac, the coloration of flamingos, a Rembrandt portrait, a Mozart quintet, all of these nourish the soul as completely as a cabbage feeds the body. Since it is the soul that never dies, this would seem reason enough.

Still, there is a hint of extravagance here, a willful waste, that unsettles the prudent mind, the mind that secretly wonders why Mary Magdalene poured that expensive oil over Jesus' feet (would not corn pads or new sandals have been more practical?) or why the Wise Men brought gifts of gold, frankincense and myrrh to the stable (wouldn't diapers have been more useful?)

Julian of Norwich saw the beauty of the world in a hazelnut cupped in her hand, because God made it, kept it and loved it. One small nut convinced her that all would be well, always. In my circumference of existence, there is a horsechestnut tree, a sentinel squad of thistles, a bevy of foxglove and viburnum bushes, all of which assure me that no matter what, all will be well. I have been advised to uproot, eradicate, cut them down because they are unproductive. They take up space which could be put to more fruitful use. What good is thistledown when you need a turnip?

I would not trade my horsechestnuts for gold or Godiva chocolates. The soft, warm feel of them, fresh from their opened burrs, in their brown, satiny skin, is a sensual pleasure. The tree itself is spacious and comforting as an

Useless Beauty • 43

earth mother, its spring blossoms a grandeur of white candelabra. And yet, what good is it? You can't eat the nuts. What do you do with them? Throw them into the fire to hear them pop? Give them to children for counters or whatever their imaginations dream up? Fondle them in your pocket like rosary beads?

Thistles are conundrums you approach with caution and respect. Awesome, intimidating, belligerent warriors, no matter where they choose to grow, they seem out of place. Their thorny leaves cut like a lance, yet their blossoms open up into the shape of old-fashioned shaving brushes made of purple silk. Then when youth turns to age, their pods burst open, and the sky is filled with dancing white down, flying off to new homes in other meadows.

The flowers of viburnum, or highbush cranberry, are another source of wonder. Large creamy white platters edged in flowerets of lace seem more suited to hang on walls as elegant china than to bedeck a scrawny shrub.

I press some blossoms in my dictionary, to marvel at when memory fades, and I leave the rest to fulfill themselves as berries. I once tried making jelly from them, and a more foul-smelling, bad-tasting mess you can't imagine. This beauty's best in the bud.

As for foxglove, have you ever looked inside their bellflowers? They remind me of elaborate ball gowns, complete with trains, with colors and designs wild as Matisse's, unique as snowflakes. No human artist or random alignment could create such detailed glory. Yet they cannot be seen at first glance; they hide away under outer wrap and, like Gray's flower in the crannied wall, often bloom unseen.

No matter how it seems, I think to judge any of these gifts "useless" shows a lack of imagination. Their potential may be awaiting the mind enlightened enough to discover it, and some already have. Over fifty years ago, Dr. Edward Bach scoured the mountains and woods of Wales for the wildflowers he used to heal emotional and physical disorders. The roots of foxglove have been found to cure heart problems and the seeds of horsechestnut to promote healthy leg veins. The undesirable cranberries provide winter delicacies for the birds.

As for the thistles, scientists have yet to find a substance within them that will be the antidote for chronic crankiness, but while I wait for that, I gather the thistledown and combine it with hops, lavender, mint and sweet annie to make a sleep pillow of unbelievable softness. I enjoy the irony.

St. Paul, who wrote his letters of encouragement to the new Christian communities (and to us) in between fleeing angry crowds, escaping jail and making tents, stuck to the basics. He exhorted us always to think on what was good, what was beautiful. Julian with her hazelnut and I with my chestnut do our best.

Foxglove

*let others expound in council,
red-capped men with golden rings
and guarded eyes,
bred in holy bookdust,
armed with footnoted
apologia to prove
that God exists*

*I need only stop
in this wood
and lift the hem
of a foxglove gown
dancing in the wind
to see such proof
as would cause Matisse to gasp,
such splash and splatter
of peacock eyes and temple bells
and swirling confetti the colors
no earthly palette yields*

*this be all I need,
this gift from One
who led me here,
who has set His seal
upon us both*

Horsechestnuts

*what good are they,
these inedible anomalies,
fruit of a tree which wears
no nest of robins in her hair,
under which no village smithy
of sound mind would stand?*

*what good are they,
if they cannot be glacéed
or chopped with giblets
or roasted on city corners
by Dickensian vendors
dispensing cheer with hot meats
in paper sacks that warm the hands
as muffs once did?*

*they are good for nothing
except to wise children
who know their worth,
who pop them from their cradle burrs
to rub the satiny skins,
warm and brown as Cassatt hair,
and be comforted
by their useless beauty*

Mrs. Yap-n-Snap

There once was a crabby, stingy old woman who lived in a shabby, dingy old house. They were both a bit shaky and shriveled and not friendly in appearance.

The children called her Mrs. Yap-n-Snap, for she was quite set in her ways, and if she didn't have things just the way she wanted, she'd yell and yap and yowl as if she had hit her thumb with a hammer.

She was at her worst when the children dared to cross her lawn, chasing their pets or just taking a short cut.

"Get off my lawn, you rapscallions!" she would yammer. "Get off my property this instant! If I catch any of you here again…"

The children fled before they could hear what she would do. They didn't want to know.

"She's so mean," they stammered and sobbed as they fell into the safe arms of their mothers.

"She's so mean she probably eats little children in a horseradish sandwich."

"She's meaner than a witch!" they all agreed.

Grumbling, muttering, snapping, sputtering Mrs. Yap-n-Snap didn't think she was mean. She thought she was just standing up for her rights.

She knew she was right about everything and everybody else was wrong and needed to be set straight. When you live alone as she did, there's no one to tell you otherwise. Mrs. Yap-n-Snap saved things. She saved *everything* — paper sacks and bits of string and candle nubs and egg cartons and rubber canning jars and corks and buttons, because you never knew when you might need them. She bought day-old bread and wore rummage-sale clothes and used an egg beater without a handle.

With her scowly eyes, sharp tongue and flyaway hair, she kept people at a distance. But once inside her house, surrounded by the things she loved, she smiled and her eyes crinkled and looked kind. It is true she loved things more than people, but it was better than loving nothing at all.

She loved her father's silver piccolo, and her mother's clock that chimed on the quarter hour, and her featherbed with its red polka-dot cover, and a music box that played "The Bluebird of Happiness."

But of everything in the whole world, she loved chestnuts — warm, satiny brown, comforting-to-the-touch chestnuts. Each fall she waited impatiently for the chestnut tree leaves to turn gold with the first frost. Then, after a good windstorm, she would rush out and gather the prickly burrs, pop them open and hold the newborn chestnuts against her face. They were soft as kitten fur.

One October day, when her lawn was covered with the tree's bounty, Mrs. Yap-n-Snap came out and picked up every single one of them. She cooed over her basket as if it were a hoard of gold. As she carried it to the house, she heard the whispering of children hiding behind the bushes and trees, a sound as sad as the sighing wind. She went inside and peered through the lace curtain on the door to see what would happen.

Slowly, one by one, the children came out, keeping their eyes on the house for any sign of the old woman. Quietly they poked and prodded the grass, but, of course, all the chestnuts were gone.

The woman watched them trudge sadly away, their hands stuffed into empty pockets. As she stood by the door, a very strange feeling was taking over her heart. She began to feel, as if it were her own, the disappointment of the children who cherished the chestnuts as much as she did.

This feeling rattled her, and she tried to shake it off. After all, the tree *was* on her property, the chestnuts *were* hers. Let the children find other trees. But the more she argued with herself, the worse she felt, and the less it mattered that she was right.

Finally, she realized she must do something she had never ever done — share what she loved. Before the sun rose, she would return the chestnuts to the lawn and give the children a chance to collect them.

"You silly, foolish old woman!" she snapped at herself. "You are only inviting them to come and destroy your lawn."

"So what?" she argued back. "So what if they walk on your, grass? Will the sky fall in? Will comets collide? Will you lose all your marbles?"

"They will never go away. They will always be underfoot." "Oh, hush, and go to sleep," she yawned and pulled the featherbed up to her ears, having the last word even with herself.

At dawn she rolled out of bed, stuck her feet into her boots, threw on her plaid bathrobe with worn-out elbows and an orange cap over her flyaway hair. Mrs. Yap-n-Snap carried the basket of chestnuts out into the frosty morning, and under the deep pink sky she flung the chestnuts in all directions, like chicken feed.

The strange feeling had grown and spread and filled every part of her, and she felt light and giddy and eager for the children to come. She made herself a cup of tea, toasted an English muffin, sat in her rocker and waited.

Before long, the children came. They scrambled (all over her lawn) when they saw the chestnuts, shrieking, pouncing, filling their pockets and mittens and hats with the precious chestnuts.

And all the while, Mrs. Yap-n-Snap was busy. She got out molasses and spices and eggs and flour and rolled out gingersnaps in the shape of stars. As she worked, she began to hum. And then she chuckled and chortled, thinking how pleased the hungry hunters would be with a platter of cookies.

She threw open the door to let out the spicy fragrance and yelled "Surprise!" and beckoned the children to come in.

At first none would come, for even though Mrs. Yap-n-Snap was acting strangely by not chasing them away, they weren't quite sure what lurked behind her door. Then one young fellow, so stuffed with chestnuts in his pockets and socks and hat that he could hardly move, said politely, "Thank you very much, but we wouldn't want to mess up your house. Why don't you bring them out here?"

And so she did. The children stumbled across the lawn and climbed up her porch and sat on her steps and gobbled up the cookies. Soon their stomachs were as full as their pockets. Mrs. Yap-n-Snap, they agreed, was not mean as a witch after all.

They whispered among themselves what they might do to thank her. Someone had an idea and passed it on to another who passed it on to another, and soon everyone was giggling and clapping with the brilliance of it.

They pulled on her apron so she had to bend down and told her what they wanted to do, whispering noisily and tickling her ear so she almost fell over laughing.

"Why, I think that would be most suitable, very nice indeed!" smiled Mrs. Hum-n-Chuckle, trying on the new name which the children had given her.

Useless Beauty • 47

*I*f the gardener looks out upon her garden with the eye of an artist, she will find enough variety of subjects to cover a lifetime of canvases. From the engineering marvel of spiderwebs hung with morning dew (turned to prisms by the sun) to the evening performances of fireflies, there is an extravagance of feast for the eyes.

Flower gardens are beautiful; we expect that. But vegetable gardens, seen with this artistic eye, are their equal. Beatrix Potter's garden at her cottage in Sawrey became a magical world through her paintings and stories, her plump carrots and cabbages every bit as enticing now as they were to Peter Rabbit a century ago.

G.K. Chesterton, in his essay, "The Aesthetes in the Kitchen Garden," says that "of all things on earth, the one perfectly beautiful thing is the kitchen garden. It has a hundred kinds of beauty richly blent into a solemn harmony. It has the beauty of embroidery, for all the colors are quiet and yet varied infinitely.... It has the beauty of a sepulchre, because so many of the shapes and colours that are seen are but the coloured crests or monuments upon the more precious bodies underground. It has the beauty of a store-cupboard, the beauty of a fairy tale...."

Within this broad canvas of beauty, there is the infinite variety of design. Some would call these examples of random alignments, "the art of chance." In his book, *Design by Accident,* James O'Brien writes that "Nature demonstrates through a combination of natural forces and materials a great variety of forms." The patterns left on the sand by the ebb and flow of the tides, dried mud-crackles, the scum on puddles that makes a marbling design, the sky effects of clouds and sunlight, all these "different designs and shapes obtained are the result of natural forces and physical laws."

Nonetheless, I prefer to call them celestial rather than accidental designs. Behind the natural order of things, there must be a Divine Order-Maker. Dorothy Gilman, in her book *New Kind of Country,* wonders, "Can anyone

rationally suggest there is no order to the universe when there are such miracles...as the way broccoli grows, designed by some celestial order to send out great leaves, and grow until it's the size of a basketball; the dark green curling leaves of spinach, ruffled like curtains; the fantastic horn-shaped flowers of the zucchini ...the silky tassels of corn?"

I would like to add to that litany the bouffant, frilly flowering kale, which looks as if it should be around an Elizabethan neck. Snowy cauliflower, whose clumping hillocks resemble the crannied landscape of the brain or a bride's bouquet. Families of peas crammed to the tips of their personal zippered pods — talk about ingenious packaging! The hexagons of honeycombs and sunflower heads stripped of seeds, like pigeon holes in a desk, awaiting their deposits.

Milkweed pods, their silky down dispersed to the wind, snapped open like discarded clam shells. The rings on tree stumps, each signifying a year of age, a design repeated at the base of celery stalks. The five-pointed stars at the center of apples and cranberries and blueberries, that mark the place where blossom turned to fruit, in the trumpets of petunias, pods of sweet anise, and even in the dry heart of logs ready for the wood stove.

But of all the designs in the kitchen garden, none delights me more than that of those distant cousins, the cabbage and the rose. The cabbage, so robust, peasanty, down-to-earth (Chesterton, with his artist's eye, says the cabbage alone has "all the colours of the sea"); the rose, elegant lady to the core, no petal out of place, dewdrops tastefully arranged. One smells of hearty soup and sausage, the other of an English garden after a summer rain.

Two opposites, you'd think. Still, the family resemblance runs true despite their divergent social circumstance. Each grows out from the heart, one leaf folding over the other, embracing, protecting, evolving into a tight bud, a solid head. It takes a knife to release the cabbage, the warmth of the sun to unfurl the rose.

Yet these opposites have united in a bit of magic called the cabbage rose. When I first saw these in a suburb of Boston, I could not believe my eyes *or* nose, for their perfume of Mozartian sweetness goes far beyond that of today's faint-hearted hybrids. "Delicious" is my word for them, these large, floppy, full-bosomed rosy apricot beauties. So how did this come about? Gardening books offer the *what* but not the *why* of the cabbage — or *Provencal* — rose, but that doesn't satisfy.

I believe with Chesterton that the garden is home to fairy tale, and that the love match of cabbage and rose is just that. If only Beatrix Potter had taken time from her naughty mice to write it!

Design by Accident

when you halve an apple
horizontally
you find twin stars,
jewels in navels
with a harem of seeds
peeking through the lattice

when you slice a green pepper
from tip to stem,
you get a dangle of shamrocks
to bless the salad

when you chop the stalks
from a celery trunk,
the stump is circled round
like age rings circling
a venerable oak

to find an oak in celery,
umbilical stars in apples,
and Trinity in a pepper
is dividend unbound,
joy nested in joy,
like the whistle buried
in a box of Crackerjack

Red Cabbage
Portrait by Breughel

imperial boulder
of Copenhagen Red,
stolid, phlegmatic,
dutifully flamboyant
Victoria in royal wrap,

tossed upon
the palette table
stained in ale and mustard
and blood of pigs and berries,
scarred by the dance of dervish knives,

you lie impassive
on your nest of dill
and burnished basil,
ignoring wood-smoke pungence
and sloe-eyed dogs drying
wet haunches by the fire,
the dance of cats scratching
to the tune of the flea,
sputtering logs and skewered meat
and fishmonger shrieks of mothers
throttling children who steal tarts,

you wait
without blindfold
for the succor of hands
seasoned with warts
and sage and garlic,
to hold you just so
for the guillotine slash

it comes,
and your regal head
succinctly halved
throbs in shock,
deepspring tears
rush to clot
the numb wound

death discards the royal robes
to bare good peasant bones,
milky limbs twinned at core
that curve to heaven
as Tree of Life

The Star at the Heart of Things

when I halve an apple,
a cranberry,
I find perfect stars
in the heart of each half,
remembrance of the moment
when bloom became flesh

today
there is the star again
in the core of the log
which feeds the fire,
five cracks splitting the dry wood,
each on its own way
to find the world
beyond home

now with opened eye
I see them everywhere
waiting to delight,
in snowflakes and starfish
and pods of sweet anise,
in the silken valleys of flower cups
and the markings of beetles,

in asterisks and cats' eyes
and the golden stars of kindergarten
stuck like jewels on the foreheads
of very good children

I think perhaps
the soul's navel
is a golden star,
lighter, prettier,
than the body's whirligig dimple,
a bon voyage kiss
from the family,
a reminder of return

Five in a Pod

There once were five peas who lived together in a pod. None of them was happy about it, for they were packed in tightly and often rubbed each other the wrong way. If one yawned or stretched or sneezed, it upset the balance, and they began squabbling and calling for the Mother Vine to do something.

The Mother Vine mostly ignored them as she basked in the sun, waiting for the mistress to come pick her plump pods. She hoped it would be soon, for Five in a Pod were getting on her nerves. Besides squabbling, the peas chattered endlessly about the grand futures they would have.

One wanted to be a Poet, another an Artist. The smallest proclaimed he would be an Explorer, and the largest said it was a Thief's life for him. The youngest said, in her sweet voice, that she would be a Nurse and make the world a better place.

The Mother Vine fluttered her leaves impatiently. "My dear children, there's no way for you to do these things. Such worlds are not for you. We are peas. We belong in the kitchen. If you want to make the world a better place, do it in soups and salads and stews. That's what peas do."

"Not me," said the Thief.
"Not me," said the Explorer.
"Not me," said the Artist.
"Not me," said the Nurse.
"Not I," said the Poet.

The Mother Vine sighed. Children were such a mystery. But it was a mystery she could not solve, so she did not dwell on it and went back to her basking.

That very day the mistress came with a basket and gathered every pod. The basket was mounded so high, Five in a Pod and some others fell from the top. The mistress left them on the road as a treat for the rabbits.

Five in a Pod hit the ground and burst open. The peas rolled across the road like marbles. They lay there dazed, their grand hopes scattered. What would happen to them now?

Instead of being eaten or trampled or run over, as they feared, each pea was picked up by the just-right person. First came a little boy, a toy sailboat under his arm, on his way to the stream. He saw the Explorer and lifted him and the empty pod up with gentle awe. What great luck — now he had two sailboats!

He ran down to the stream and set his toy sailboat upon the water and then the pod with its Captain Pea. The pod wobbled slightly. Then the current caught it and carried it swiftly past the sailboat and out of sight. The little boy waved good-bye to it.

Soon the stream disappeared into a river. Then the banks faded from view, and the river became part of the ocean. Waves swirled and churned and finally deposited the pod onto a grassy shore. The Explorer sank wearily into the warm earth and went to sleep.

Within days, a slender vine pushed out from the dirt bed, inching its way toward a coconut tree. It climbed up the trunk and wound itself around it, and when the vine blossomed, people came and marveled at this wonderful gift brought by the sea. They ate its sweet green fruit, and what they did not eat, they saved as seeds to plant in their gardens. Soon peas were as common to the land as dates and bananas.

Meanwhile, the other peas were having their own adventures. A painter searching for blueberry fields came along the road and almost stepped on the Artist. He picked up the pea, studied him carefully and brought him back to his studio.

He arranged the Artist on a blue cloth, directly in front of the mouth of a salmon. Behind the fish, a silver vase held a bouquet of celery, dill and rosemary. When he finished the painting, which he called *Still Life with Pea*, the painter popped the pea into the salmon's mouth and baked the fish to flaky perfection. Then, with much pleasure, he ate it. So while the Artist ended up being eaten after all, at least he was immortalized in a great work of art.

The Nurse fell into the hands of a boy who had a habit of picking things up off the road. Then he forgot about them. The Nurse, swallowed up in the darkness of his pocket, was sad. How could she make the world a better place while nestled next to a dead worm?

She wasn't there for long. The boy had been blowing pebbles through a peashooter, trying to knock down an old wasps' nest. When he ran out of ammunition, he remembered the pea and, after much searching in his pocket, found her.

"One more shot, and you're gone, wasps' nest!" He blew so hard his ears popped. The Nurse flew high up in the air, over telephone wires, and into the rain gutter of a house across the street.

A bedroom window looked out onto the roof, and from her bed of decaying leaves in the gutter, the Nurse could see an old woman bent over a table cluttered with scissors, tweezers, pots of paste and velvet scraps. In the center sat a huge dictionary, its pages lumpy and crammed with dried flowers and ferns. The woman turned the pages carefully, now and then lifting fragile wisps of pansies or forget-me-nots or whatever she needed to create a portrait on the velvet.

Before long, the Nurse's vine pushed out from the gutter and made her way to the window. Now she could have a good look! She found herself looking straight into the delighted eyes of the woman.

When the vine flowered, the window seemed to be covered with a flutter of tiny white butterflies. The woman, who could no longer venture out to pick flowers in the field, rejoiced in the blessings that had come to her. She picked all but one of the blooms and pressed them in the dictionary, in the section reserved for rare specialties.

As for the pea who would be a Poet, he was found by a writer who had gone for a walk because his brain was tired. With furrowed forehead and eyes cast down, he searched the ground for ideas. When he saw the pea in the middle of the road, he stopped and smiled at such a silly thing. And yet it was true. He scooped up the pea and hurried home, certain it had a story to tell.

That night, as the writer worked, eating a peanut-butter-and-honey sandwich, a blob of honey fell onto the pea and stuck it to the manuscript. When the writer went to bed, he put the manuscript under the mattress, in case burglars might come in the night and steal his priceless thoughts.

He spent a terrible night, tossing and thrashing about and getting tangled up in the sheets. The next morning, as he removed the manuscript, he discovered the cause of his discomfort. It was the pea!

Being a frugal writer, who used every scrap of experience for his stories, he sat down and wrote a tale about a sensitive princess and an annoying pea. From that day, the Poet occupied a privileged place next to the writer's pen and inkwell, as a reminder that even something as small as a pea has possibilities for greatness.

Now only the Thief remained on the road, and he was miffed by this fact. Of all of them, he should have been found first, for was he not the largest, loudest and grandest pea of the five? Yet there he sat, overlooked. He hoped he would be found before sundown when the rabbits came out.

Suddenly he saw great puffs of dust coming toward him and heard the sound of flying feet, then a shriek and a thud.

A small wiry fellow sprawled before him, his nose almost touching the pea. They looked at each other and knew they were kin.

"Are you a robber?" asked the pea, brashly addressing the human.

"That I am, and a good one, too. More of a gambler, really," said the man with pride.

"May I join you? I have much to learn."

"It would be a pleasure," said the robber, and he flicked the pea into his purse.

The two became comrades in crime. They worked together in a game played with walnut shells. People would bet on which shell hid the pea. Of course, they never won, because the gambler's hands were too quick. But the robber grew cocky and careless with success and was thrown into jail (with his accomplice) for cheating the Chief of Police.

The shock of losing his freedom changed the gambler's way of thinking. When he left prison, he became a minister and traveled the country lecturing on the evils of gambling.

He told about his life as a trickster and held up the pea, which he said he would carry with him forever to remind him of his sad, bad past.

The Thief was not entirely converted. He missed the thrill of the chase and the delight of outwitting everyone. But he did enjoy the traveling and the attention and figured it was better than a short life in a stew.

And that is the story of Five in a Pod, who got what they wanted but not exactly as they had imagined.

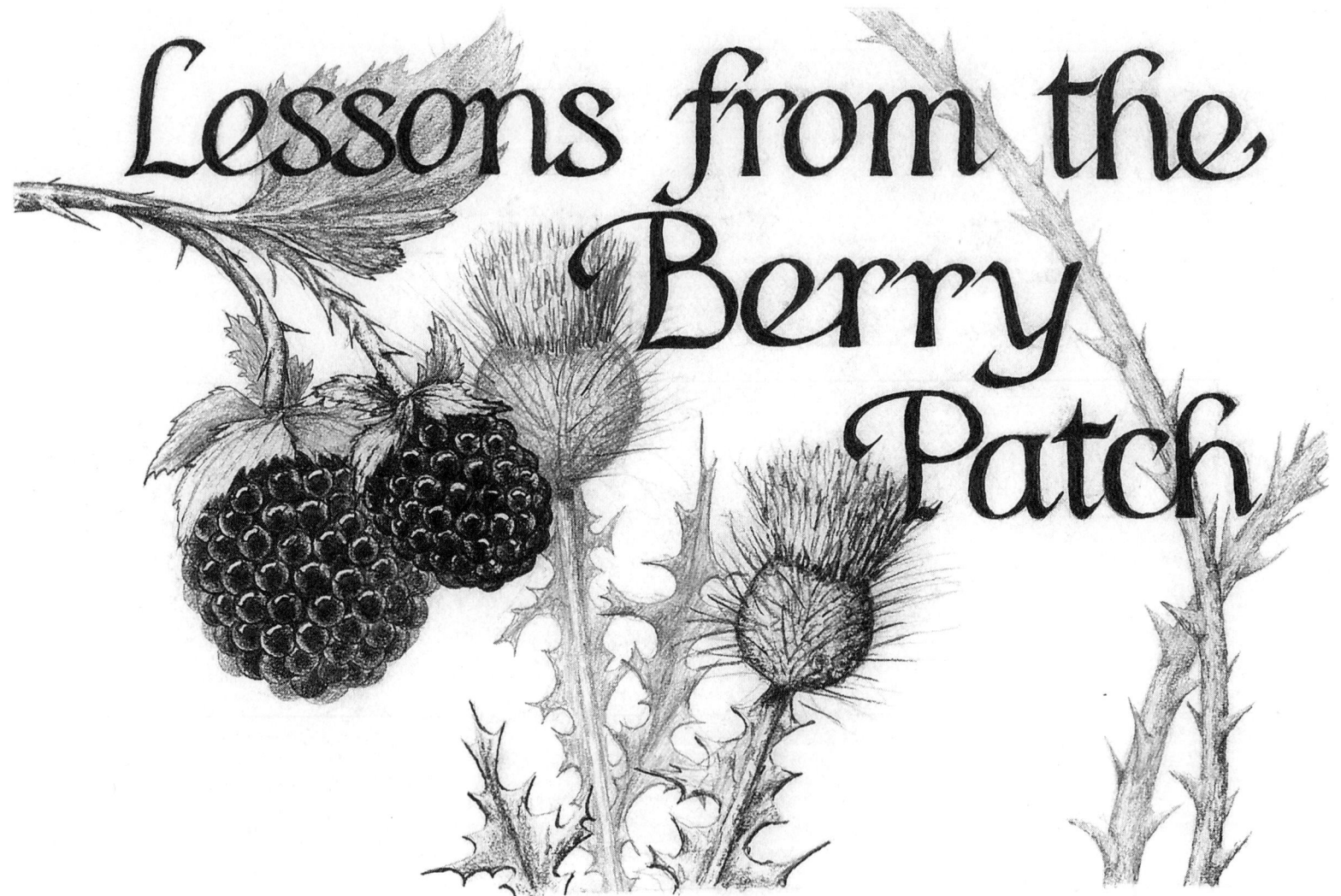

*I*f life on earth is a no-nonsense school which pummels us into enlightenment, then the berry patch is where we do our graduate study. This course is not for timid hearts or those who fear pain, bugs, slippery slopes and sudden storms. Berriers are adventurers vaulting out into the unknown on faith, like the apostles going off into strange lands, knowing there is a harvest to be reaped but not quite sure where, when or how. Still, they go because they must.

I think berry-pickers are born with this special gene, which is probably in the shape of a strawberry. They are as passionately obsessed with the process of hunting, picking and jamming as are painters, poets, plumbers and truffle-hunters with their passions. It's a gift; it cannot be acquired but may be passed on. Sadly, few of my children have it. To this day they bemoan their harsh childhood of enforced berry-picking. (My memory is that they ate more than they picked.)

For me, berry-picking is high adventure, right up there with raising children and writing stories, that brings out the best and worst in me. It hones the virtues of patience, perseverance, endurance and humility (especially when I fall and spill an almost-full bucket of berries.) It also exacerbates my selfishness, greed and quick-tempered anger — an anger that erupts when I discover someone else has been there already, trampled the canes and picked the vines clean. How dare these marauders violate *my* sanctuary! (I choose to forget that God does not label his beneficence for specific pickers, and that God always provides a sufficiency for all. I learn, slowly, to accept and go on. Another patch awaits.)

Overriding all is gratitude to the Creator who led me to this feast. If God is so thoughtful in such small delights,

Lessons from the Berry Patch

how can we doubt that he is forever within the heart of the big challenges? "I give you berries because you desire them," he says. "Trust me for all the rest!"

There is a woods fringing my almost-acre of land, and I count these woods as part of my garden, which has always been rebellious of borders. Here God treats me to a munificence of wild berries — strawberry, blueberry, gooseberry, red raspberry and, my favorite, blackberry. (Raspberries are the prettiest of all when the sun shines upon them and turns them into translucent crimson jewels, like the hard candies that fill Christmas stockings.)

Blackberries test the mettle of the berrier. Robert Tristram Coffin writes that the only way to pick blackberries is in a tank. Not having a tank, I make my own prudent preparation with a long-sleeved shirt that buttons at neck and wrist, bug spray, clippers to cut away dead canes, hat to prevent wasps from nesting in hair, sneakers with laces double-knotted so I won't trip on them. I tie a gallon bucket around my waist to leave my hands free. With a prayer to St. Anthony to guide me and my guardian angel to protect me, I am off with pounding heart to climb my Everest.

I maneuver past giant tree roots and fallen rotten trunks where snakes like to snooze. Little skittery animals rustle under leaves, and porcupines, quills aquiver, watch me from nearby trees. Wasps hover menacingly about my face, their long legs dangling casually, as they decide which part of me to sting.

Once inside the patch, there is pain. The thorny vines reach out like witches' claws to rip my sleeves and arms beneath, and there are moments of claustrophobic panic as I try to wrestle free of them. Soon it is hard to distinguish bloodstain from berry on face and hands. What price glory -- the fresh pie baked for supper!

I notice that on the old brittle canes of little shabby bushes, leaves already yellow and wilted, grow the plumpest, sweetest, large-as-thimble berries. So often we bypass the old in our hurry to get to the new. I notice that when I think I have picked every berry, I haven't. When I turn around, approach the bush from a different angle, I see the lush ones I missed, hiding under the leaves. Even in the berry patch, what you see is not always the whole truth. Circle around, examine from another perspective, and you find more fruit.

The writer Ray Bradbury describes heaven as a house with the porch light on. How fitting that is, the image of the beacon light guiding the weary seeker through the dark, the wintry storm, up the stairs to that door which when flung open lets loose a merriment of laughter, shouts of welcome and warm bearhug embraces of reunion!

Now I think of the celestial woods beyond that house and the delight therein — an endless berry patch hung heavy with fruit under a perpetually August blue sky, without thorns or wasps or snakes, where every seeker's bucket is filled to overflowing and not one berry is spilled. This too is heaven.

Blackberry and Thistle

A thistle seed carried on the wind landed in the dark, moist soil of a wood, right next to a blackberry bush. It was a comfortable spot and to her liking, so she settled in and put down her roots. She was unaware that no plant had ever shared the spot with the bush, for he would not allow it.

Wild gooseberries and cucumber vine, even woodbine and golden rod which grew anywhere, tried in vain, but the blackberry bush kept all trespassers at bay. He did tolerate some scrub pine and alders, which had already been there when he was just a shoot, and since they ignored each other, they got on reasonably well.

Over the years, the blackberry bush had grown to a large and menacing size. Its thorny limbs reached out like witches' claws to grab whatever they touched. Many a bear and human seizing upon its fruit left whining, with scratched limbs and noses.

The blackberry bush enjoyed his fearful power. He was quite full of himself, and since no one would dispute him, he considered himself lord of all growing things in the wood, if not the universe.

And then the thistle seed came and dared to grow right beside him! From the first rosette of prickly leaves that appeared, the blackberry bush was both annoyed and curious. What arrogant thing was this, to grow so close he could touch it without even trying?

Each day the thistle grew taller, standing strong and perfectly straight, its sharp-toothed leaves spreading like a fan around it. Soon it was almost as tall as the blackberry bush, who decided it was time to act. He threw his raspy, curling vines around the thistle but drew back in quick pain as he caught himself on her thorns.

"Kindly keep your distance, sir," the thistle spoke coldly, her words dropping like sharp little icicles. "In the land where I come from, thistles are honored for their stalwart courage. 'None Dare Provoke Us' is our motto. You had better consider that."

The blackberry bush had never been spoken to like that. He bristled and blustered. "*I* keep my distance? It is *you* who has invaded my home, and I would like *you* to leave it now!"

"Absolutely not," she laughed. "The wind brought me here, and here I stay. I find it quite comfortable, despite a certain neighbor. Now, would you kindly keep quiet while I enjoy the afternoon sun?" And she turned away from him haughtily.

The blackberry bush, speechless, pretended he didn't care and turned away from her. From that time on, he ignored the thistle as much as she would let him. And when her green pods opened, he was doubly annoyed, because all day long the bees and hummingbirds and butterflies flocked to sample the nectar of her purple flowers.

"That noise is driving me to distraction," he grumbled. "There's no peace around here any more."

The thistle sniffed, "I'd rather have these winged ones around me than those four-foot clods you attract."

"I get the two-foot ones too. They won't have anything to do with you," he retorted with a hint of pride.

"They're just as bad," she said. "Raccoons, hedgehogs, humans — what a bunch. You're welcome to them!"

And so it went all summer, back and forth, neither giving an inch to the other, both absolutely certain of the rightness of their opinions. The blackberry usually came out the worst in any argument because he had the least patience.

"You always have to have the last word," he would sputter angrily.

"No, I don't," she would smile smugly.

In August, when the crickets first began their singing, the farmer's wife came to collect her bounty of blackberries. She dressed for battle, wearing one of her husband's old flannel shirts, buttoned tightly at neck and wrists, a red kerchief tied around her head, a white plastic bucket tied around her waist.

She knew that her hands and face would get scratched and bloodied and that a thorn would stick in her thumb which she would have to pick out with a needle, but the lure of fresh blackberry pie for supper was so strong, that she plunged fearlessly into the thicket.

She groaned with delight at the sight of branches bowed down with ripe berries the size of thimbles. Already she could feel the grasp of the thorny vines clinging to her back and tugging at her kerchief, but she thrust her arms uncaring into the heart of the bramble.

Bits of thistledown caught onto her shirt and went into the pail with the berries, and she stopped to admire the bursting pods of silk. She had seen the purple blooms earlier and thought how much they looked like her husband's shaving brush. Now they had turned into this magical fluff.

"How beautifully soft it is," she thought. Then, being a farmer's wife who used everything, she decided to gather the down. She took off her kerchief, tied it at the corners, and made it into a pouch. She cut open the thistle pods with the clippers she always brought to cut away old blackberry canes, and stuffed the kerchief with all the thistledown it could hold. Some escaped and floated away to begin new lives in another field.

The next day the farmer came and cut down the blackberry bush, the thistle and the alders and scrub pine to clear a space to store the fence posts for spring. Around the fence that would be built, thistle seeds would sprout and the blackberry root buried deep in the earth would send up new shoots, and all would grow up together as equals.

In winter, the farmer's wife would watch the snow from her rocker, spread blackberry jam on her toast and rest her feet on a purple pillow filled with thistledown, marveling that things so soft and sweet had come from such a prickly tangle.

Elderberry Jelly

they came as gift
in brown paper bag,
oozing and embarrassed,
knowing the housewife
had wearied of jampot froth
and washing dead spiders
from mustard and honey jars,
knowing they were summer's afterthought,
bland black mush to the tongue,
sought by none but beggary birds

yet the thrifty housewife
grumblingly accepts,
and alchemy begins
water runs blue
in the cleaning rinse,
blue as sky streaked leaf green,
blue juice simmered,
strained through gauze,
pours purple, cold deep
coffin-draped purple,
purple syrup boils,
churns, foams, thickens

sheets of scarlet flood
into jars turned jewels
in the September sun,
humbling even the wizard

so also do we change
with the chemistry of our days,
litmus to circumstance,
shaken, plucked, rinsed,
crushed, strained to the bursting,
brought to a full rolling boil
that cannot be stirred down,
simmered to essence caught
and kept with sealing wax

I wonder if at end of day
God holds us up to the light
as the housewife does her jelly,
determining our excellence

The Gypsies' Tale

Once upon a time a young gypsy and his wife grew tired of the traveling life and came to live in the deep wood. They cleared a spot of land near a spring that had bubbled and gushed before there was a wood, and they built a cottage big enough and small enough for them to be happy in.

It had a thatched roof and pretty windows with pots of parsley on the sills and a root cellar for the turnips and beets they would grow in their garden. Brambles of wild blackberries ringed the cottage and kept back the forest; and alongside the house, near the kitchen window, grew a young cherry tree.

In the spring it danced in the wind like a young girl, shaking its white blossoms as if they were curls. When the gypsy and his wife watched from the kitchen window, they laughed to see such a thing; and the tree, like a true performer, bowed when they clapped their hands. And when they sat beneath it and the petals fell like April snow into their mugs of tea, they could hardly speak for the sudden beauty of it.

The cherry tree fed not only their spirits but their bodies as well. In summer they picked baskets and buckets of fruit, and each year the crop grew larger and the branches bowed more heavily with the tree's bounty.

The birds of the deep wood came and helped themselves to the fruit at the very top, where the gypsy and his wife could not reach.

"Let them have them," said the gypsy to his wife, who was a little put out at not getting every single cherry. "The birds are gypsies like we are. The earth is their mother too and shares her gifts with us all. Why do you ask for more work than you need?"

The woman knew he was right. So she forgot about the birds and started making the pies and tarts and jams to sell at the weekly market in the village. Here she also brought bunches of herbs and horseradish roots for colds and a salve for boils that she made from beeswax and pine resin and garlic.

Her husband, who could do a little of everything, came with her and spent the day shoeing horses and patching pots and pans for the women of the village. Sometimes he was paid in money, sometimes in bits of this and that. He refused nothing, for he saw possibility in every cracked piece of pottery, every broken bead, every length of tin or leather.

After market day they would come home tired but happy, eager to sit under the tree and exchange stories of how they had used their wits. But first they would bathe in the wooden tub by the spring, washing themselves with oak leaves in the icy water, listening to the birds putting down their children for the night.

And so the years passed, and as you might expect, the gypsy and his wife and the tree grew older together. Their limbs stiffened, and they were less able to bend and dip with the playful wind.

The blossoms of the cherry tree were scanty now, and its bark was rough and peeling. Still, it did its best for the couple. It still gave enough fruit for a dozen pies and one batch of jam, which the wife saved for themselves.

Then a very hot, dry summer came upon the deep wood, when even the animals lay down under the pines and panted. They were too hot to play games or fight or dig holes. The spring no longer gushed but trickled to a whisper, and the gypsy and his wife could get only enough water to wash their faces and make their morning tea.

The poor cherry tree, thirsty as well, still loyally put forth its meager crop. It was not surprising that the birds began to eat the cherries, all of them, even those on the lower limbs. The gypsy's wife shouted and banged her pans to shoo them off.

"Do something about those birds!" she ordered her husband. "Look, they have eaten clear down to our cherries. They will leave us nothing." She began to sigh and cry loudly and wipe her nose on her apron. The gypsy put his hands over his ears and tried to think.

Finally, he went into the wood and in a little while brought back strands of young, wiry grapevine. He got out his box of odds and ends, and dumped the dishes and silverware and prisms and pipes onto the kitchen table.

The next morning he went out to the cherry tree and hung six wind chimes on it. The chimes clanged and clinked and rattled and rippled, making music that never before had been heard in the deep wood. And as the gypsy hoped, it frightened the birds from the tree, so his wife was able to pick enough cherries for two pies, one to sell and one to eat.

In time the autumn winds blew on the tree like a trumpet, and all the leaves fell, and the chimes hung naked for all to see. The prisms and glass beads sparkled in the sun, and the string of old cups with violets painted on them clanged gently. The flattened spoons and forks rang like dinner bells, and the wind sang softly through the dangle of tin whistles.

The birds flying overhead saw all this and now knew they had nothing to fear. The curious things made music just as they did, but not as true or pure. They sat on the branches next to the chimes and twittered and caroled their bird song along with them. Even in winter's snow they came, the cardinal and blue jays and foolish nuthatches hanging upside down.

The gypsy's wife was touched as she watched them giving so freely of their song, expecting nothing in return.

"We must get some suet when we go to the village," she said. "The birds are hungry."

"I do not understand you, woman." The gypsy sighed, shaking his head. "First you tell me to get rid of the birds. Now you want me to feed them."

"There is nothing wrong with feeding birds in winter. They can't eat the cherries then," she said.

"You're absolutely right," said the gypsy, knowing he would never get the better of his wife.

And they hung the suet, which the wife had stuffed with millet and thistle seeds and cranberries, next to each of the wind chimes. The birds flocked to the tree, in such numbers you would think they were its blossoms, and put on a splendid show of song and aerial tricks, as if to say thank you.

When spring came, the tree bore only five cherries, which the couple ate mournfully on a summer's evening.

The years passed, the gypsy couple grew older, and the cherry tree gave no more fruit. But the couple never forgot the tree's generosity of its youth.

One summer evening, the birds gathered together and chirped long and intently, as if conferring. The next morning they congregated beneath the gypsies' window, making such a commotion they woke the old couple.

Startled, the gypsy and his wife hurried outside and watched the chattering birds, time and again flying off and then returning. A cardinal flew directly to the woman's feet and tugged on her nightgown with his beak.

"I think they want us to follow them," said the husband. His wife agreed. Quickly they changed their clothes, and followed the birds, pushing past the bramble thickets, the wooden tub, and the gushing-again spring; past the fairy rings and brooding pines and vines of wild grape — so thick you could swing on them — deeper and deeper into the wood where they had never gone before.

Finally, they came out of the dark wood and climbed a small hill into a clearing. What a sight awaited them! Dancing in the sun was a grove of young cherry trees, their satiny barks glinting, the ripe, crimson cherries dropping in clumps to the ground.

"Ohhhhhhhhh," said the gypsy's wife. "I have never seen such cherries! Where did they come from? How long have they been here?"

The cardinal, already busy in the tree, answered her question by plucking a cherry and dropping it to the ground Then he dropped another, and another, until the cherries lay in a row as neat and orderly as the trees themselves. The gypsies watched with their wise eyes, and understood everything.

And so the gypsy and his wife picked cherries until they ran out of containers in which to carry them. The woman filled her apron until it overflowed, and the gypsy did the same with his shirt and hat. They would have to come again, for there were enough cherries left for at least one hundred pies.

That night, by the light of the waxing moon, the gypsy's wife planted a cherry pit alongside the dying old tree, so that in a few springs she could once again watch the merry dance of the cherry tree from her kitchen window.

There is a comfort in certainty, and in the garden proper we have certainty. We know that when we plant a rutabaga, we will get a rutabaga. We know that we will, if we are lucky, reap exactly what we sow, and that is a pleasurable satisfaction.

But there is that little squiggle of divinity in the human soul that cannot settle for comfort. We crave mystery, the tingly unknown of the road not yet taken. Like the chickens in the barnyard who yearn to soar with the wild geese, we want to escape the familiar and go into the woods where adventure awaits. We need the heart-thumping exhilaration of being "surprised by joy," as C.S. Lewis puts it.

To seek this surprise, we set off with no expectations, no destination, no script, no thought but to meander and be open to whatever calls out, "Look here!" In her book *Zen Gardening* Veronica Flay writes, "all you have to be is open. Whenever you go to the universe with an empty bowl, it is always generously filled."

I go with a basket rather than a bowl, and a pair of clippers, nothing more to weigh me down. Often the surprises that await cannot be caught and confined to a basket. Sometimes it is music — an intricate trill of birdsong, or the wind in the willows (and birch and elm and maple), rustling the leaves like a thousand tiny tambourines. Sometimes it is fragrance — lilies-of-the-valley or thyme or lemon mint underfoot, or the combination of apple and cherry blossoms, or the funky, musty whiffs of valerian, reminders of dirty socks kept too long in the hamper.

Sometimes it is the landscape of wildflowers, waving meadows of orange devil's paintbrush, purple loosestrife, spiky bluebonnets, Queen Anne's lace, an army of pink lupines marching down a hill — a palette lush enough to rival Monet's real garden at Giverny.

Even if we can't carry these joys home in our hands, we bring them back nonetheless in every pore and molecule of our souls, passing them on in the way we think and laugh and love. There should be a special word for the osmosis of beauty!

More often, our bounty is tangible. There are wildflowers to gather for making winter tea, the wildlings of every season, from spring violets and fruit blossoms, wild roses, poppies and yarrow, to the last straggler red clovers of fall, all are picked and laid on a sheet in the attic to dry. As with mushrooms, the rule is to pick only what you know to be safe. Beauty and fragrance can be deceptive (lily-of-the-valley and buttercup, for instance, are poisonous.) If you have any doubt, *don't*. By November the dried flowers are ready to make into a golden amber brew. Add what you wish — orange or lemon rind or cinnamon — to suit your taste. I like it just as it is, with a teaspoonful of honey and a heart full of *thank you*.

Dandelions are better in wine than tea. Their golden heads turn white and fuzzy in old age and add nothing to flavor. But if you come upon an unfurled blanket of them crying to be picked, you can make a conversation-piece dessert from them:

Rhubarb Pie with Dandelion Topping

    4 cups cut-up rhubarb
    2 cups sugar
    4 tbl. flour or cornstarch
    2 tbl. butter

Put all this together in an unbaked pastry crust. Then make the topping: Into a blender put

    ½ cup cream or half & half
    1 egg
    2 tbl. flour
    yellow petals from 40 dandelions

Blend for one minute and pour topping over rhubarb. Sprinkle cinnamon and nutmeg on top. Bake at 350 degrees for about 45 minutes or until top is flecked golden-brown.

I use the flowers of yarrow and comfrey in making a salve to draw out boils and skin infections. It has been in my mother-in-law's family for generations, handed down from her ancestors in Alsace-Lorraine. The recipe is quite old, and I've had to adjust it, such as substituting ½ pint Pure Gum Turpentine (obtained from a hardware store) for "1 lb. Lump Turpentine." And I have added the flowers because they are good for cleansing wounds.

Mother Logel Salve

    1 lb. yellow beeswax
    ½ pint pure gum turpentine
    5 lbs. lard
    17 cloves of garlic
    17 pinches of salt
    7 slices rye bread (without seeds)
    handful yarrow and comfrey flowers

Boil everything together until the bread is brown as toast. Discard the bread. Pour mixture through a cheesecloth-lined sieve and then into small containers (baby food jars are just right). Cover and store in a cool, dry place.

I have used this for my children and cats for years, and all have lived to tell the tale.

The clover heads that don't go into the tea I use in making Homemade Honey. This doesn't have the natural healing qualities of true honey, although clovers do purify the blood, but if you don't have the real stuff on hand, this will do nicely:

<u>Homemade Honey</u>
24 white clover blossoms
12 red clover blossoms
handful of rose petals
scant tsp. of alum powder
2 lbs. white sugar
1½ cups water

Boil for 4 minutes. Cool and use.

I am intrigued by the specificity of these recipes in using *40* dandelions, *17* cloves of garlic, *12* red clover blossoms. What would happen if I was careless and let an extra petal or pinch slip by? Would the salve grow mold? Would the honey turn gummy? I'll never know, for I don't mess with what works.

On the other side of the woods there is a field of lacy wild mustard, the kind that if you had faith the size of its seed, you could move mountains. I pick just enough to dry and sprinkle into salad dressings. Usually nearby is its good companion, horseradish. Now for this, you must come with a spade and be prepared to dig to China to unearth its pungent roots. There will be great groaning, of both earth and digger, but for the hard-core horseradish lover, it's worth it, strained back and all. Freshly, tearfully, grated into Dijon mustard, spread on pumpernickel and Swiss cheese, it is Ambrosia of the Cleaned-Out Sinuses Gods!

The little wild apple trees, whose blossoms spread like pink sea foam in the springtime, give double pleasure in the fall, with the scarlet nuggets dangling like jewels from their bent old limbs. They aren't good for eating (unless you don't mind biting worms in half), but they are perfect for making cider and pomander balls.

Pomanders are a grandmother thing—sweet, spicy remnants of another era, worked over at weekly sewing circles with strong patient fingers and used to freshen up closets and hope chests. They are made by covering the apple, round and round, completely with whole cloves. Then it is coated with powdered orris root, usually by shaking it in a paper bag, wrapped lightly in tissue paper and put away in closet or drawer to dry. Pomanders last for years, and even when they have turned to fragile, paper-thin husks, their fragrance warms a room. Like grandmothers.

No matter what the season, we return with our bowls overflowing with the day's catch of surprise. Of all the gifts an indulgent Father gives us, my favorites are the unexpected, undeserved ones of grace, wonder and surprise. The very words make us smile and say, "Well, isn't this amazing?"

I think God enjoys surprising us, catching us off guard, keeping us on our toes for what may be around the corner.

There may be angels unaware dancing in the meadow, so be alert! If God were a writer, I think he would be O. Henry, for they are both masters of the surprise ending. As we near the climax of the simple (divinely planned) story, we, with our superior intelligence, think we have it all figured out.

Then we turn the last page and have our socks knocked off by a twist in the tale, a serendipitous confluence of events so clever, so marvelous, so *right*. God and O. Henry go beyond filial connection. They are soul-brothers.

Pomander

*round and round the rosy skin
I pierce a crown of cloves
over and over again*

*the freshsprung juice
oozes through the cobbled spice
and trickles down my fingers*

*like blood drops rising
to protest the thrust
of rude thorns*

*I wash my hands of the sticky mess,
but the sweet-smelling stain
will not leave*

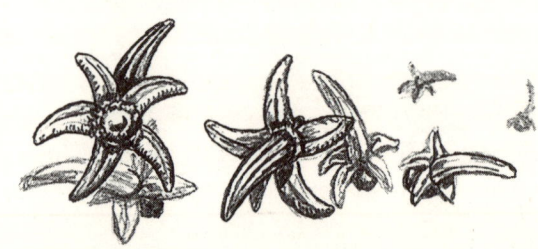

Pressing Cider

it was as if
the windows of heaven
had flung wide and loosed
the torrent of discards
rolling, rumbling,
bouncing, bruising, jostling,
spinning cartwheels,
leaping like frogs

into the hopper,
oblivious to outcome
as red-cheeked lemmings,
go these huddled masses,
refuse of ancient orchards
abandoned to worm
and desperate deer,

within the crucible
Blue Pear and Pippin,
Cortland and Mac,
Baldwin, Spy, Sheepnose,
and the small winter apples
of Thoreau's delight
give up the ghost
in sputtering snap,

pressed down, shaken well,
and once again for good measure

ambrosia foams,
blushing, rushing pink
overflows to flood
and burst the burlap dam,
and in its wake
stunning bees,
who go unresisting
to sweet demise

Wildflower Tea

One sunny Monday in May, an old man went out with a basket in one hand and a walking stick in the other. He strode briskly along a country road until he came to a stream. There, he stopped and stood very still, watching the shadows of the quicksilver trout beneath the water.

He stopped to caress a white stone polished smooth by the water, and there, by the toe of his shoe, he spied some violets, their faces turned up to his.

"Please pick us up," they seemed to be saying, and so he did — every white, yellow and purple one of them, until his basket was full.

He returned home and climbed the rickety stairs to the attic. There, on an old table covered with a clean white sheet, he emptied the basket of its treasure.

One cloudless Tuesday in June, the man packed a lunch of canned sardines, dill pickles and crunchy cookies, and went to the meadow where the wild strawberries grow. He carried two baskets this time — one for the berries he would pick for jam and shortcake, and the other for the blossoms of an abandoned orchard.

Fringe Benefits • 73

When he was a child, he had climbed these trees, and picked plums and cherries and apples. Ancient now, they bore no fruit and were almost forgotten. Nobody came here except the old man, who saw more than the scrawny limbs and gnarled trunks. He saw, too, the host of pink and white flowers flung to the sky, like whimsical ribbons on old ladies' heads.

First, he got down on his old knees and picked every berry he could find. Then he shook the branches of the trees and caught the flurry of petalfall into the other basket. Weary, he stretched out under an apple tree, ate his sardines and pickles and cookies, and then went happily home with his bounty.

One bright Wednesday in July, he got out of bed, wrapped a chunk of cheese and a heel of pumpernickel bread in a red scarf, put on a straw hat and hurried down the road like a spool of unraveling thread.

He started to climb a cliff near the ocean, eager for the prize awaiting him atop the crag where seagulls dined on clams. Along the way, he snipped the heads of wild thyme and lemon grass and pasture rose and edelweiss, small and white as the feathers of a baby snow owl. Finally, he reached the top, where the clouds seemed near enough to touch.

Blueberry blossoms bowed in the noonday breeze, like nuns in sunbonnets praying. The old man heaped his basket full with the flowers (and three stowaway bees, drunk with nectar) and ate his bread and cheese there on the threshold of heaven. After a bit of a nap, he brought his basket home, and freed the bees who had just awakened.

One muggy Thursday in August, in the late afternoon, when the sky unveiled a skeleton moon, the old man set out for the shore. Sprigs of peppermint and leeks hung from his hat to ward off mosquitoes, and from his belt dangled a large tin bucket, a knife for cutting away brambles and a dented tin cup. He clanged like a tinker selling pots and pans as he slid down the bank to the sandy shore, still wet from the tides rolling off to foreign lands.

Here, he found the crimson beach roses, like royal ladies wrapped against the spray in satin kimonos. They had been brought from the east long ago, in sea captains' cargoes of nutmegs and lace and ivory fans.

He picked up all the petals the bucket would hold, and then, as mist turned to fog, he stumbled into a blackberry briar, hung heavy with ripe berries as long as his thumb. He filled his cup with them, and ate many more. Then up the bank he carefully climbed — he could not lose a berry or rose — and followed the path home, lit by fireflies.

One cool Friday in September, the old man put his garden to bed. He said good night to the parsley and poppies and cornstalk sentries, now silent and brittle as crisp toast.

Here and there lingered the wild friends who had come to visit and stayed — red clover and purple catnip spires, yarrow and mallows and other stragglers who didn't care a bit that summer was over and continued to bloom. He picked them all before covering the garden with a quilt of leaves, then carried them in his cap into the house.

Up to the attic he went, past a row of sleeping bats, and emptied his harvest onto the sheet, on top of the mountain of other dried and dying blossoms.

One crisp Saturday in October, when a chill was in his bones, the man put on a sweater with a hole in one elbow, and went out with his basket to search for winter apples.

As he walked past crowds of wild asters and Queen Anne's lace and goldenrod and Michaelmas daisies, he imagined he heard the drone of bagpipes, and of cheering and applause. On both sides of the road, the blossoms crowded and clamored and seemed to wave as he passed.

So touched was he, he forgot about apples and picked the autumn blooms instead. They too were brought to the attic now sweetly hung with the spice of old flowers, so like the fragrance of his mother as she rocked him, holding him close, shutting out care.

One chilly Sunday in November, when the logs burned red and warmed the man to his toes, he rubbed his hands with joy and said to himself, "It is the time; the time is right to brew my special tea."

From the kitchen shelf, he took a large golden tin splashed in red and green and blue designs, and gently pried off the lid. Off it came, and an explosion of color and fragrance burst from within. The man breathed in deeply — of rosebuds and mint, of sunny meadows and salty cliffs, of streams in no hurry and the sound of bagpipes. Here were the wildings of spring and summer and fall, mingling with each other, no longer flowers but tea.

He brewed his tea in a blue china pot, poured it into a chipped white cup with forget-me-nots on the handle, and dropped in a dollop of honey and of cream. He sat by the window, cup in hand, watching the first snow fall.

"I am," he sighed deeply, "contented as a clam. I am a most happy man."

Hercule and Dijon

In an abandoned pasture in which cows once grazed, there lived two unlikely friends. One was Hercule, a horseradish, and the other was Dijon, a mustard plant. Both were wild things, brought to this meadow by wind and circumstance, and here they thrived in sun and solitude.

Their friendship was of the spirit, for they lived in two different worlds. Although they were nourished by the same soil, Hercule grew beneath in the dark clods of earth, his strong, thick limbs stretching out and tunneling so far they reached another country, while Dijon reached toward the sky in a lacey bush topped with hundreds of golden flowers.

She conversed with Hercule through his headdress of green plumes, telling him of the bluebirds and clouds and mushrooms that lived in her world. Hercule responded to her roots, which were sturdy enough but nothing like his, describing the moles and grubs and occasional beetles that visited his dark world. They listened to each other graciously, never interrupting. Nothing was too insignificant to share — the landing of a Monarch butterfly on the mustard or a sudden rainstorm that bowed her down or the wet droplets sparkling like jewels when the sun came back.

Hercule could only imagine the brilliance of sunlight, and he did not think he would like it. He loved his life in the dark, the good rooted feeling of being master of his universe and not subject to the whim of wind or rain. But, of course, he did not say this to his friend. Instead he told her of the joys of tunnel-making and the satisfaction of quiet persistence. Dijon could not imagine being imprisoned forever in the dark — how depressing! But, of course, she did not say this to her friend.

The days passed, with their good-natured exchange of opinions and reporting of news below and above. Occasionally, there would be an invasion of the pasture by others, usually loud, sudden, and mercifully short-lasting. Children and their mothers came to picnic and pick wildflowers to press in their dictionaries, play hide-and-seek and climb the gnarled apple trees. Dijon once had quite a scare when a little girl was about to pick her flowers, but her mother said, "No, they aren't pretty enough — how about some Johnny-jump-ups?" That was a narrow escape.

And once Hercule was quite shook up when the earth rumbled under the flying hooves of horses and dogs pursuing a fox who often visited the pasture. In their mad rush, they trampled most of his plumes, but enough were left so he could still hear Dijon's anxious voice. Eventually he grew new leaves and was his old self again.

Near the end of summer, new owners bought the pasture and decided to grow blueberries on the land because the soil was right for it. So one day when there was no wind, they set fire to the field to destroy the burdocks and thistles and alders that had taken over. Dijon was terrified, for she had never seen fire. She watched the flames lick closer and closer to her and Hercule. For the first time, Hercule felt himself a prisoner, unable to escape and protect his friend. He could lose his headdress and still survive, but Dijon, uprooted or burned, would die.

Then, unexpectedly, a soft rain began to fall and kept the fire from traveling farther. Despite a few singed leaves, Dijon was unharmed. She held her sunny head high to catch the rain and then told Hercule every detail about the fire — who was left standing and who was not.

A few days later, as Dijon was describing how thistle silk had gotten caught in her blossoms, an old man and his wife came into the pasture. Dijon reported their movements to Hercule, "I don't think they're the new owners: I've seen them here before. They're very sweet together — he holds her hand and helps her over the rocks. The old man has a shovel and the woman has a basket. They're walking towards us."

The couple stopped before the horseradish and the mustard plant and nodded to each other. The old man dug his spade swiftly and deeply into the dirt around Hercule. He jumped onto the spade to make it sink even deeper, and then, with much groaning and reddening of his face, he brought up his bounty — Hercule, or most of him. "Couldn't get it all," he gasped, "but that's all right. Leave some for next year, right?"

The old woman was busy with her knife, cutting away Dijon's flowers and leafy sprigs. Then off they went, the autumn afternoon sun turning the sky purple, Dijon in the basket and Hercule in a sack thrown over the old man's back. This is the end, they thought sadly, of a beautiful friendship.

But it didn't turn out that way. That very day, even before supper, the old woman stripped and chopped and cooked the mustard with water and vinegar and spices, while the old man scrubbed and grated the horseradish and added it to the mustard. The sharp, heady smell made their eyes blink and fill with tears.

"Well," said the old woman, blowing her nose, "that'll clear out your sinuses. But won't it taste good on our sausage?"

She put the snowy gold mixture in a small brown crock and set it in the center of the table. She thought it looked every bit as pretty as a bunch of summer pansies.

Hercule and Dijon felt a bit awkward now that they were together, as pen friends do when they finally come face to face.

"We meet at last," said Dijon shyly, wishing Hercule could have seen her delicate branches dancing in the wind.

"I would have known you anywhere," said Hercule, wishing he could have impressed her with his strong limbs of which he was so proud.

Then the couple sat down to their supper of sausage and potato and cabbage, covered lavishly with the golden spread. With each bite, through their tears, they sighed with satisfaction and marveled over this perfect blending.

*I*n the center of this dining room table where I write, there is always, from spring to Halloween, the perfect bouquet. It is ever-changing with the seasons, as are its containers of china cream pitchers, tea pots, cranberry glass or black-lacquered vases, but it is always perfect.

Unlike surfers seeking the perfect wave, skiers the perfect snowy slope or singers the perfect pitch, creators of the perfect bouquet don't have to be highly skilled, disciplined, physically fit or intensely focused, They are not perfectionists, nor are they obsessed with rules or limits.

For the creative arranger, there are no rules. You simply gather what you find, a little of this, a lot of that, until your hands can hold no more of the catch of the day. Then you bring the bounty to the kitchen table for decision-making. What you do with it is up to you. Eye and hand are your guide to the challenge of choosing the complementary container and presentation.

In the process, a bit of magic happens. A surprising compatibility emerges in the community of strangers as diverse as characters in an Agatha Christie mystery. Pinks and reds, weeds and wild grasses, respectable perennials, haughty lilies, peasanty phlox, all blend and mingle in a harmonic congeniality.

Once spring really settles in, the kitchen becomes workshop, laboratory, palette and canvas. It is awash in sweet fragrance and Easter egg pastels. Tulips, daffodils, narcissus, lilac, iris — all sturdy, dramatic and easy to work with. They are proud, steadfast and do as they are told. By summer, the parade of flowers is lush, extravagant, almost too much to pick. The table is heaped with variety: the down-to-earth cottage garden crowd — canterbury bells, snapdragons, primroses, bluebells, delphinium, the fragile-stemmed bachelor's buttons, coral bells, gypsophila, tufts of baby's breath and blue lobelia, and the lovely, indispensable Queen Anne's Lace, the filler that sets off any bouquet.

The Perfect Bouquet • 79

Some flowers, I accept, do not play well with others. They need their space. Asian lilies, for instance, really stand out when each is given its own slender vase. They need this as much as a hermit needs his cave. My favorite solitary bouquet is that of a burgundy star lily, preening itself over the rim of a green glass wine bottle labeled *The Poet's Corner*.

There are also some flowers that do not grab my fancy. Gladiolas may be your delight but they are not mine, nor are most spikey blooms. Some I admire set in their native hills and slopes but when brought into my inside world, they go limp and pouty and weep for their homeland. And I am not inclined towards the large, extrovert, pushy blooms, like dahlias, peonies or sunflowers. Sunflowers especially intimidate and tend to take over a room. I wonder if Van Gogh, after he painted his mesmerizing beauties, allowed them to stay in his tiny bedroom.

By fall, most growing and flowering has stopped. Flowers found now are treasures, rare and valued. Yesterday, the weather word was for a killing frost. Tomorrow, everything, except the nose-thumbing brussels sprouts, will be blackened desolation. So I make my final foray to pick the stragglers and hardy innocents that remain. Red clover, calendula, marigold, the last of the nasturtiums, even one lone, confused dandelion, that blooms to a different drummer, and the last hollyhock flower, a late-bloomer low on the stalk.

The hollyhock becomes a hat for the Mary statue, a frothy pink skimmer that should lighten her heart. In a few days, it will begin to shrivel and cling to her head like a bathing cap. Then, paper-thin and dehydrated, it will become a hat again, a remembrance of summer past, which Mary will wear even on Christmas Eve.

As a last gesture, I pick a poppy bud, still tightly furled in its green sheath, but if I squint, I can catch a glimpse of its red promise. I have little expectation, for I have no luck with buds cut before their time. Roses, peonies, chrysanthemum buds have all died on me, their cocoons turning to shrouds, so none but God would ever know the beauty within. Still, it would surely die in the frost, so I will try again.

This morning when I came downstairs, I saw a splash of scarlet in the porch window framed with pumpkin and goblin lights. The poppy had burst open, sometime between last night and now, without benefit of sun or warmth, and was blooming its brilliant little heart out.

Outside there is the expected desolation, the bare, black trees, the wind whipping the brittle leaves into hysterical mobs fleeing down the road. Inside, I drink my coffee, contemplating the marvel and perfection of this singular survivor. Sometimes there is a sweet satisfaction in meddling and having it come to good.

Meddling

> "I realize today that it is a mortal sin
> to violate the great laws of nature…
> we should obey the eternal rhythm."
> —Zorba the Greek

'tis the last incipient rose of summer
I've not left to bloom and die
in the foretold frost
I have cut it unborn
to force its birth
in the window vase
into a pallid life of limited span,
unreal as a mannequin's smile,
but life nonetheless, I reason

despite my good intentions
and the cheery midwife sun,
will it die stillborn
in its green shroud?
and if it does,
will I learn not to play God?

Sunflowers

I pick them young and round
as saucers cupped to catch the sun
whose daily trace they emulate

I cut them at noon,
heads and stalks precisely plumb,
stand them in a wide blue vase,
a plump, motherly sort, yet stiff-necked
enough to keep them in line
one leaf escapes the rim,
droops disarmingly like a child's curl

I bring them to the pleasant room
crammed with disorderly books,
yellowed photos in silver frames,
dozing cats, eyes half-alert,
yogurt raisins in a pink bowl
on a lace doily

perceptibly, there is a chill
flowers so innocent in the garden,
so dwarfed by sky, loom now overbearing
in lesser domain, arrogant gods
with madness in the marrow,
demanding obeisance

in such alien light,
the room turns poor
I see that nothing matches
the footstool leaks sawdust
white curtains are grey
fingerprints smudge the candy bowl
I see that the cushions abandoned
by wary cats are threadbare

only if you live in a manor
or have tamed lions
should you let sunflowers in

Still Life

narcissus crowd the narrow vase
like schoolgirls jamming
the convent window
to watch a parade

smaller ones
hug the lacquered rim,
petals smoothed back from their faces
like the ears of a cat annoyed

while tall ones hover
in the bouquet eye,
nun-elders
gently restraining
lest a giddy one fall

The Late Bloomer

There was once a hollyhock who bloomed so late she was the only flower left in the garden. Her mother had already settled into the roots for winter hibernation, which made the hollyhock feel a bit odd and unwanted, growing up without a mother. Her siblings had already flown off with the wind to begin a new existence elsewhere, and she had no friends to share gossip or wind dances or sun baths with. Outside of a few heads of cabbage and a stand of brussels sprouts, the garden was gone by, bereft of past glories.

One day after a hard frost, a little girl came out of the house looking for anything that might have survived, wanting to gather a bouquet for a statue of Mary and the Child. She picked a few feathery plumes of asparagus fern and a sprig of yellow tansy beads. That was it, she thought, the last flowers for Mary until the first snowdrops of spring.

Then she saw the bright spot of pink hiding under a large hollyhock leaf. It was a perfect, unblemished flower, blooming as if it were the middle of summer. It was, she told her mother, a miracle.

They could find no vase small enough to fit the tiny stem, so the little girl plopped the hollyhock upside down onto Mary's head. A special flower deserves a special place, she said. Her mother agreed, admiring the elegance of the wide-brimmed gauzy skimmer with scalloped edges. "Now Mary can go to a tea party whenever she's invited," she laughed.

After a few days, the sunshade brim began to shrink. The hat grew smaller and clung to Mary's head like a pink silk bathing cap. It was so tight it seemed as if it were painted on. Weeks passed and snow covered the garden, and the hollyhock grew even smaller, until it sat shakily like a pink beanie on top of Mary's head. "Very soon," thought the little girl's mother sadly, "Our Lady will outgrow it completely."

That very night, the new kitten was on the prowl exploring and jumped up to investigate the niche in the bookshelf that was the statue's home. He rubbed against Mary and his exuberant tail knocked the hat off and down to the floor.

The hollyhock rolled around like a top and finally stopped under a rocker, which fortunately was not in use. This was all very bewildering to the flower, who had gone directly from garden to statue and knew none of the perils of life beyond that.

A mouse mother, out on her nightly rounds of picking up some groceries, had seen the kitten before he saw her and hid behind the couch. She watched the tiny hat fall and roll to its resting place, and as soon as she heard the kitten pad upstairs to the little girl's bed, she came out to survey the situation.

She examined the hollyhock, wondering how she might use it, for she was a practical and creative mother who never let anything go to waste. When she sniffed the summery fragrance lingering on the flower, she knew exactly what she would do with it.

The mouse carried it home, squeezing it and herself carefully down the hole in the floor beneath the kitchen sink and then got out her sewing basket and a scrap of white flannel with red hearts on it. She cut it and sewed it into a large heart (large for a mouse, that is) and stuffed it with sprigs of lavender, hops flowers, and the hollyhock. Then she wrapped it in tissue paper as a Christmas gift for her youngest child, who was nervous and twitchy and needed help getting to sleep.

The hollyhock found her new home comfortable and the lavender and hops flowers very congenial. At last she had found the friendship she had longed for in the garden. Once she had wondered why she had been born to bloom alone and unseen. Now she realized there was privilege in being the last as well as the first of anything.

The Garden in Winter

*I*t is December, and the garden is dead. Anyone with eyes can see that. No life stirs beneath or above that snowy shroud. No vines or rows of vibrant greens, no teeming busyness of workaholic bees, no butterflies on the phlox. No birdsong but the raucous triumph of crows ferreting tidbits from the compost, blue jays making rude remarks and mourning doves lamenting the state of the world.

The Christmas tree, its moment of glory past, huddles in a corner outside the kitchen window, waiting to be of use in spring. Limbs will be sawed off and linked together, like friends arm-in-arm in a photo, to make a support for young pea vines. Now abandoned spider webs dangle from the tree with their catch of dried leaves.

In the garden proper, clumps of brittle poppy and tansy stalks stand, bending into each other like old biddies sharing gossip. The lattice fence has disappeared beneath the snow, leaving the black metal Scaredy Cat on its own. It seems to be on a trek across the tundra, always in mid-walk, never moving. The Glitter Owl in the tree, twisted this way and that by the wind, casts prisms of scarlet and purple and gold onto the snow in a kaleidoscope of colors. I never noticed this in the lushness of summer.

It's hard to deny what our human eyes and rational mind tell us: The garden is dead and committed to memory. But we know there is more to truth than what we see.

As Little Buttercup sings in HMS Pinafore,

> Things are seldom what they seem,
> Skim milk often passes for cream....

Our physical eyes show us a one-dimensional reality, but our eyes of faith confound earthbound assumptions. As Advent leads us to Christmas, as the embryo becomes the born child, so too this plot of deathwhite silence continues to live and grow in its own Advent sleep.

We know in our innards there will be resurrection and joy in the morning, come spring. All will be well and divinely ordered. Hummingbirds will hover over the bee balm, bees will get drunk in the valerian, the black cat will resume his role as sentry, the real cats will roll ecstatically in the emerging catnip. And before we know it, we will once again be drowning in zucchinis.

The true gardener accepts winter with equanimity. No point in muttering or grumbling or sighing. As Karel Capek writes in his book *The Gardener's Year*, "Against the winter weather, nothing can be done. No zeal, no ambition, no newfangled methods, no meddling or cursing is of any use; the germ opens and a sprout comes up when it is time, and a law has been accomplished. Here you are humbly conscious of the impotence of man; soon you will realize that patience is the mother of wisdom."

So while the snows pile up, I, more or less patiently, pore over the garden catalogs. They begin to arrive in January, a trickle at first; then, by March, the mailbox is crammed with horticultural offers I can't refuse. My mind becomes sodden with too much of everything — there is nothing that is not "amazing!" "incredible!" "unusually rare!" and prolific enough to feed the world. My brain feels as though that 300 lb. miracle pumpkin is growing inside it.

The order list is written and rewritten after many scrutinies. Do I really want rainbow beets — can I handle blue borscht? And what about red carrots and cranberry-speckled beans, white eggplant and pink banana squash? In the end I usually scratch these in favor of new flowers I can't resist. This year it's Blue English Wood Hyacinths, Hungarian Breadseed Poppies and Pink Ruffled Daffodils.

Then there are the ritual resolutions, as impassioned and unattainable as ever. Still, I persist. A woman's reach must exceed her grasp, or what's a heaven for? *This* year the garden will be neat and weedless. The rows will be straight and orderly, not serpentine. I will make paths with little white stones from the beach. There will be an aesthetically pleasing twig fence around the garden. I will invest in a Great Horned Owl with Rotating Head. I will place a statue of St. Elizabeth of Hungary in the circle of breadseed poppies. And the scarecrow will go. In its place will be last year's Christmas tree, wonderfully preserved beneath winter's snow, and I will plant pea seeds around it for a late-summer crop. As its needles brown and spill and give off its dividend of flavor, the old tree will be born again in a shimmering of green vines and white blossoms.

And I will indulge in the compensatory delights of winter, those pleasures foregone because of my summer obsession with earth. Now is the time to read and write and visit, make patchwork scarves and rag rugs, bake lemon meringue pies (the urge brought on by the sight of swirling snowdrifts), and I will enjoy the morning iceflowers on the porch window panes.

The ghostly beauty of these crystalline paintings is, I know, a scientifically explainable phenomenon. Karel Capek says that "to make them flourish...the windows must not shut properly; where the wind blows into the window, flowers of ice will grow. They flourish more with poor people than with rich, because the windows of the rich shut better."

Yes, that is the *how* of it, but what explains the artistry, the detailed intricacy, and the fact that these are identifiable plants? "Their foliage," he writes, "resembles endive, parsley, celery, teasel, fern and other plants with spiny, feathery foliage." I also see silvery thistles and Icelandic poppies dancing with each other, with a sprinkling of doves overhead. More, I see God's imprint on these improperly shut windows.

Hans Christian Andersen said that his life was a fairytale writ by the hand of God, and I think that is true for us all. With what deft hand he arranges us just so, in this village, with those parents, and these gifts and flaws and brilliance or lack thereof. God the storyteller and artist paints the stories of our lives as he does the iceflowers on the porch windows, each day a fresh start, a new fairy tale determined, shaped, by the cracks and circumstances of the day, and every one a masterpiece of ephemeral and eternal beauty.

The Whiteness of Meringue

"The whiteness of meringue becomes for me of great poetic preoccupation; it's like snow, like frost...like purity."
—Artist Wayne Thiebaud

*so that's it,
why, when I see drifts of snow
caught in frozen waves
against the snaking fence,
twirled in crusted peaks
glassy in the sun,
a primordial need,
unreasoning as geese flying south,
thrusts me into the kitchen
where windows steam from
simmering pea soup,
and cats hog the heat
from hot-air registers*

*and I, a driven woman,
hunt for the double boiler,
break open eggs, prick the crust,
whip the whites to creamy peaks,
cocoon the lemon heart
in mounds of purity*

*then, having done my part,
transfer power to the oven
and wait for art
to reflect life*

Random Alignment

"Heaven and earth are threads from one loom."
—Shaker proverb

*Twelfth Night past,
the Christmas tree
discarded outside
my kitchen window,
shorn of ornament
save remnant flutterings
of tinsel,
faces into the wind,
bemused, unruffled,
like dispossessed royalty
denying the coup*

*soon
a meringue of snow
frosts it prettily,
layers of sleet
sheathe the limbs
in amniotic ice,
preserving each needle
in singular perfection,
like bees in amber*

*all the while
from the gutter above,
an icicle thick
as a wrestler's
inches towards the treetop
in singleminded relentless yearning,
closer and closer
with each day's balance
of freeze and thaw*

*until a whip of bitter wind
molds the icicle melt
into a finger gently bent
to grasp the goal,
like the finger of God
reaching for Adam*

*in such meeting
heaven and earth
meld as seamless
one*

Iceflowers

*iceflowers bloom
on midnight glass
above the stove
which sleeps now cold
and white as death*

*overwhelm the pane
in splashy spray
of lilies and fern
and oak leaves wreathed
into silvery scrolls*

*and skittish doves
who rise and hover
like broken halos
above the cobwebbed Madonna
guarding the sill*

*iceflowers defy
the morning doom,
as the sidewalk artist
brandishes his chalk
at thunderclouds*

*despite bravado,
dawn decrees —
the iceflowers wilt
in an exodus of tears,
and giddy doves fly south*

*breakfast heat
removes all trace
of enchantment,
the window no longer canvas
but medium of what is*

True Love Never Dies

One bitter cold night, the worst of the winter, Jack Frost or some other itinerant artist who worked in ice, outdid himself on the porch windows of a farmhouse.

While the world slept, he created an exhibit which would have made any city gallery proud. On nine windows were paintings of the commonplace — snowflakes, pine trees, ivy scrolls, lacy ferns — but in each of the three remaining windows, huddled together in a triptych, there was a story.

In the center window, a tall, princely man with a plume in his helmet looked down upon a slender woman, lovely in her billowing gown. He asked her to dance; she agreed. They clung to each other as they danced, he stiff and proper, she leaning back somewhat, savoring the moment. The first streaks of sun turned her gown to crimson and his plume to purple. Far off in a corner of the window, a peacock bloomed royal blue.

In the window on the left, a young woman sat at a small table by a window, writing on a piece of paper. A white cat sat on the edge of the table, contemplating the lace curtains frozen in motion.

In the window on the right, two angels flew to heaven arm in arm, leaving a flurry of doves and stars in their wake.

When morning came, the children, their eyes still cobwebbed with sleep, their fingers turning blue with cold, stood in speechless delight at the panorama. They had to be coaxed into the warm kitchen to eat their oatmeal with cream and brown sugar crusting on it. "Don't worry," their mother said, "it's so cold outside, they'll still be there when you're done."

But she had forgotten how strong the sun could be, even in winter, and how snowflakes melt in a flash on the tongue. As the children ate, the handsome young couple whirled together one last time in a blur of brilliant color, until their bodies melted into a trickle which spilled over onto the window sill. "Never fear, my darling," cried the young man while he still had a face, "true love never dies!"

The angels, shining like gold now, knew they would not reach heaven, but, being angels, they just laughed merrily and waved good-bye to the stars and doves, who were already fading. "Don't worry, my dears, we'll all be back. True love never dies!"

In the picture with the writer, the lace curtains went first, sparkling as if they had been strung with sequins, and then the cat, as if he had just slipped from the table. The young woman barely had time to finish her letter to her beloved — "Dearest, no matter what, true love never dies!" — before everything, desk, paper, inkwell, the young woman, disappeared.

The pictures were soon forgotten by the children, now eager to rush outside and leave their mark on the untouched snow. The daylight world of snowplows and mailboxes and barking dogs shone bright and clear through windows now cleared of all enchantment.

Many months later in the summer, if the children looked closely at a patch of meadow flowers beyond the garden, they might have seen a slender poppy in a scarlet kimono, dancing with a stalwart thistle of such regal bearing that he towered above all other flowers. The dancers regarded each other so tenderly that the butterflies lined up to watch and refused to bother them for nectar.

And below the meadow in the apple orchard, they would have seen two newlywed doves in their nest, singing soft, sad songs to each other. Then the doves would dash off for a carefree soaring, playing hide-and-seek and follow-the-leader. Such activity was unusual for doves, but then, they were newlyweds.

As they swept through blossoming apple trees, they set off a petal fall of fragrant snow, which the wind caught and tossed like stars to the sky. Doused with petals, the doves cooed, "Never have two doves, two anything, been so in love!"

And if the children had looked up at the farmhouse, they might have seen their sister, a budding poet, writing at the table by her bedroom window, staring past the curtains, searching for a perfect word. She wrote with a quill pen, the feather tickling her chin. Then she dipped the pen into an inkwell, holding it poised in the air, ready for inspiration, should it come. A black kitten sprawled on the edge of the table, trying to knock over the inkwell.

The sheet of paper before her contained one line: *A thing of beauty is a joy forever.* She thought this an appropriate subject for a summer's day, even though she suspected it wasn't an original thought.

She looked past the lace curtains and the black cat to see the dancing flowers and the flurry of petals stirred up by the giddy doves, and the sweetness of it all poured out through her pen.

Out of nowhere, as if some angel had dropped the words into her mind, the young woman wrote and underlined: *True Love Never Dies,* which, she reasoned, was almost the same as *A Thing of Beauty Is a Joy Forever.*

Her pen kept dipping and writing, as if it had a mind of its own, and before she knew it the sheet of paper was covered with swirls and flourishes and i's dotted with tiny circles. She was quite proud of what she had written and how it looked on the paper and how all the lines rhymed with "dies" — flies, cries, skies, butterflies — and all so effortlessly. She knew she had been truly inspired.

The young woman blotted the paper, folded it, put it into a pink envelope, sealed it with a red wax heart, and mailed it to her one true love.

The Garden in Winter

Recycling

when it is time
for me to leave
this old house
I have molded to my comfort,
this outerwear worn
threadbare smooth to perfect fit,
throw a goodbye kiss,
lock it into memory,
level it to ash
in quantity to fill
a mayonnaise jar
and several coffee cans

then on a spring day
of gentle wind, or in October
when the maples blaze gold,
bestow it on the gardens,
the old lilacs and thistle hill,
the wildflower patch on the leach field
and the woods I haunted for berries,
around the horsechestnut trees
and the little house where I wrote poems
and watched the generations of
big fat spiders repeat their mothers' lives
in the upper right-hand corner of the window,

and every other place I worked and sat
and pondered the mysteries of slugs
and difficult children
and what the Pope really believed
and if Brahms and Clara Schumann
ever consummated their love
and what to have for supper

do this in memory of me
and I'll come back
in the crisp, feisty pickle,
the scarlet silk of gypsy poppies,
the wild sweetness of blackberry pie,
the chestnut you fondle
and cannot throw away,
the rose that finally
blooms

The Fruitcake

Many years ago, a young boy gave his mother a fruitcake for Christmas. It was small and round and dark, crammed full with nuts and fruit and spices. It was tightly wrapped in cellophane and packed in a pretty blue tin with a stagecoach embossed in white on its cover.

When his mother opened it, and the fragrance of nutmeg and cloves escaped the tin, she said it was the most beautiful fruitcake she had ever seen, and the son knew he had chosen well. It had cost him three dollars, a large sum for a small boy, but it was worth every penny, seeing the pleased look on his mother's face.

Now, in truth, the mother did not really like fruitcake, and neither did his brothers and sisters. But she loved her son and would never hurt his feelings, so she said, "You know, this is such a special fruitcake, I would hate to waste it on us. Once it's open, we have to eat it up. I'd like to save it for when we have visitors and need a special treat." And everyone agreed that would be fine.

The mother set it up on a shelf in the pantry, where it would wait for unexpected company. But when company did come, they brought sausages and cheese or tuna casseroles or pizza, and after they had eaten, everyone would be too full for fruitcake.

By the time the next Christmas came around, the fruitcake was still waiting. But it was still sweet to smell and moist to the touch, and the mother said, "We'll have it with eggnog on New Year's Eve." But the children wanted popcorn and root beer instead, and that is what they had.

So it went, year following year, the fruitcake sitting patiently in its spot next to the cookie cutters and nut grinder and pot for melting wax. The mother thought about it now and then, but she had been told that fruitcakes keep forever, so she was in no hurry to use it. The boy had forgotten about it. Now he gave his mother potholders and aprons for Christmas.

The family moved several times, and each time the fruitcake was carefully packed and went with them onto a new shelf in a new pantry. Occasionally the mother would lift the lid and touch the cake to see if it still felt alive. It seemed to have gotten smaller and shrunk away from the sides of the tin. She wondered about the mysterious ingredients inside. Were they still plump and vivacious inside the home they had never left?

Many years passed, and the children grew up and moved away, even the young boy. One year he came home for Christmas (now he gave scarves and perfume as gifts), and the mother set him to work rolling out gingerbread men. When she reached for the cookie cutters, she saw the blue tin, still waiting patiently. She brought it down and set it on the table.

"Remember this?" she smiled.

"Oh no," her son laughed, "not the fruitcake!"

The Garden in Winter • 93

"I think it's time we did something with it," she said. She broke open the brittle cellophane and lifted the shrunken cake from the tin. It was very, very light and yet very hard.

The mother got out her sharpest bread knife and tried to cut a slice. It wouldn't make a dent. "Let me try," said the son, using all his strength. Nothing happened. The cake seemed to have turned into petrified wood.

The son went to the barn to get a saw. Back and forth he worked it over the cake, until his face grew red and sweaty and he had to take off his flannel shirt.

"What shall we do?" asked the mother, disappointed that after all these years, she would not get to taste the incredible fruitcake.

"I have an idea," said the son. "follow me!" He gathered up two hammers, some chisels and an ice pick, along with the fruitcake, and he led his mother out into the garden. They stopped at the statue of St. Francis, cemented into the frozen earth, a withered zucchini vine wrapped around his waist.

They set to work with hammers and chisels, attacking the cake, pounding for all they were worth, until finally it fell apart into four chunks. The mysteries within had been amazingly preserved. The cherries were red, the citron green, the nut halves intact, and the faint fragrance of spice lingered over the bare garden.

"Imagine," said the mother, "this fruitcake is 25 years old!"

"Imagine," said the son, "this must be how scientists feel when they discover a million-year-old fossilized flower!"

They arranged the chunks around the statue, wondering what birds or animals would want to eat them.

"I'll bet they'll still be here in spring," laughed the mother.

But she was wrong. The fruitcake was quickly covered by the first snowstorm of January, followed by many more and leaving layers of blankets piled one on another, like quilts on a bed. "Maybe the snow will soften it," hoped the mother.

When spring came and the snow melted, the pieces were gone. Not a crumb, not a cherry, not a nut remained. "It is a mystery," she wrote her son that night. "What on earth could have happened to them?"

She could not have imagined. The animals and birds who came to the winter garden to scavenge the compost or any little green shoots that came up in mild spells had been puzzled by the strange, unyielding gift left by the humans. Several crows had damaged their beaks by futile blasting. Intrigued by the sweet fragrance, some raccoons and skunks gnawed away in frustration, becoming only hungrier in the effort.

"It's no use," was the word passed among the creatures. "It looks like food, it smells like food, but it isn't food. Forget it." An owl with a reputation for trivial knowledge said they were meteorites.

Yet there were a few who looked at the puzzle with different eyes and found the fruitcake useful. The woodpecker took away a piece, which he whittled into a cradle for his new daughter. The woodchuck scurried away with another, which was exactly the right size to finish the foundation of his new home. The rat rolled a piece out of the garden, down to the stream bank where he lived. He spent the winter fashioning it into a dinghy for summer fishing.

An old dog with poor eyesight passed by and sniffed at the last piece. An old bone, he thought, and was very excited because he hadn't had an old bone for a long time. He picked it up in his jaws and trotted off happily to bury it in his place for special treasures.

The mother wondered about the fruitcake now and then as she worked in the garden that spring. She hoped that after spending 25 years on a pantry shelf it had gone on to a more exciting life. If she only knew!

The Garden in Winter